WHAT TO EXPECT WHEN GOD PURGES THE HEART

of
ex-Boyfriends, ex-Husbands,
ex-Lovers and Former Relationships

WHAT TO EXPECT WHEN GOD PURGES THE HEART

of
ex-Boyfriends, ex-Husbands,
ex-Lovers and Former Relationships

Copyright

© 2020 by Sabrina M. Stephens, All rights reserved.
ISBN: 978-0-578-64643-5

Printed in the United States of America

All Rights Reserved. This book or any portion thereof may not be reproduced or used in any form or any manner whatsoever without prior written permission of the author, except for the use of brief quotations in a book review or as provided by the United States of America copyright law.

Unless otherwise noted, all Scripture quotations are from the New International Version and the Living Bible Version of the Bible.

Scripture quotation noted (NIV) are taken from The Holy Bible, New International Version copyright 1973, 1978, 1984, 2011, by Biblica, Inc. Used by permission. All rights reserved worldwide.

Scripture quotations marked (NLT) are taken from the Holy Bible, New Living Translation, copyright © 1996, 2004, 2015 by Tyndale House Foundation. Used by permission of Tyndale House Publishers, Inc., Carol Stream, Illinois 60188. All rights reserved.

Scripture quotations marked (TLB) are taken from the Holy Bible, The Living Bible Version copyright © 1971 by Tyndale House Foundation. Used by permission of Tyndale House Publishers Inc., Carol Stream, Illinois 60188. All rights reserved.

Commentary references come from the Holy Bible, Life Application Study Bible Version, copyright © 2011 by Zondervan. All rights reserved.

Book Cover Design, T. Jones Media, hello@tjonesmedia.com
Book Editing and Formatting, Sabrina M. Stephens
www.sabrinamstephens.com

Dedication

This book is dedicated to my family and friends.
Thank you for keeping the Word of God in my ear!

This book is also dedicated to Warrior Nations Ministries
We are the 99 going after the 1
One Million Souls for Christ

The Great Commission

Then Jesus came to them and said, "All authority in heaven and on earth has been given to me. Therefore go and make disciples of all nations, baptizing them in the name of the Father and of the Son and of the Holy Spirit, and teaching them to obey everything I have commanded you. And surely I am with you always, to the very end of the age."
Matthew 28:18-20 (NIV)

Acknowledgments

The Greater Piney Grove Baptist Church
Atlanta, Georgia, Years 1990-2000

Total Grace Christian Center
Decatur, Georgia Years 2000-2005

The Intercessors of Total Grace Christian Center
Decatur, Georgia Years 2000–2005

Intouch Ministries
Landmines in the Pathway of the Believer

John Hagee Ministries

Suggested Books to Read

Spiritual Warfare
Biblical Truth for Victory by Chuck Lawless

Liberty Savard Ministries
Shattering Your Strongholds and Breaking the Power

Imprisoned by Secrets of the Heart by Patricia C. Harris

Why Kingdoms Fall by Bishop Paul S. Morton

Pigs in the Parlor (The Practical Guide to Deliverance)
by Frank and Ida Mae Hammond

Contents

Part 1
- Chapter 1: Case Scenario: A Woman in Crisis
- Chapter 2: The Ex Factor
- Chapter 3: 7 Points of Wisdom
- Chapter 4: The Truth is the Light
- Chapter 5: Identifying the Problem, Resolving the Issue
- Chapter 6: Relationships Work Best When God Establishes Them His way!
- Chapter 7: The Sin Trap
- Chapter 8: Triggers
- Chapter 9: Understanding the Difference, Love, and Lust
- Chapter 10: No More Secrets
- Chapter 11: Rely on the Holy Spirit

Part 2
- Chapter 12: What does Purge Mean?
- Chapter 13: Why is Purging Necessary?
- Chapter 14: God Purges the Heart for Three Reasons?
- Chapter 15: Purging Targets the Soul
- Chapter 16: Expect a Change in Attitude and Actions
- Chapter 17: Expect a Change in Motives and Intentions

Part 3
- Chapter 18: Purge My Heart, I'm A Woman in Crisis
- Chapter 19: Ouija Board: A Demonic Game of Lies and Deception
- Chapter 20: Idolatry. What Will You Do?
- Chapter 21: Surrender (Your Life for His Glory)
- Chapter 22: 8 Benefits to Expect When God Purges the Heart

PART I

CHAPTER 1

CASE SCENARIO A WOMAN IN CRISIS

It was my first day as a Personal Worker at my church. My role was to talk one-on-one with a person after they'd responded to the Pastor's invitation for salvation, restoration, or church membership. I was one of many on this ministry team. On this particular day, I sat patiently waiting for someone to be assigned to me. Soon, a young woman came into our room and was directed to sit in the available chair facing me.

She was a Caucasian woman, probably in her late 20s. She identified herself as a Christian and wasn't seeking restoration or membership. This soft-spoken woman was on a serious mission to get help though. I found her to be sincere with a dedicated and devoted heart for Christ, but she was confused and conflicted and needed guidance and prayer. She didn't hesitate or hold back in any way as she told me exactly what was bothering her.

This young woman had a personal dilemma. She was single but felt she was still in love with an ex-boyfriend who was reaching out to reconnect with her. The problem was he was married to someone else, and after a year of being married, he wanted to rekindle his relationship with her. Needless to say, understandably, her emotions were all over the place because she still loved him. Her affections for him had not subsided after their relationship ended, not even after she learned he married another woman.

She was feeling compelled to follow her heart and go back to him. She was talking with him regularly and giving in to the pressures of his pursuit, along with the desires in her heart and mind towards him. She wanted him back and was about to let him know.

The Holy Spirit led this woman to sit with me of all people. As soon as she started talking it was like hearing myself talk five years earlier when I came to this very church in distress and needing help. My emotions were out of sorts, my behavior was out of control, I was totally out of character and in big trouble [spiritually] back then. I was in spiritual warfare, yet I didn't even know what that meant at the time. In addition to the warfare, God was purging my heart by dealing with emotions I had buried a long time ago. He was also revealing to me a propensity to sin when given a specific opportunity. This woman was me, except God had already healed, delivered and purged my heart by this time. I had finally surrendered to his will above my desires. I was no longer dealing with past issues but, ironically, she was re-telling my story (at least a story very similar to mine).

She and I are not the only two women in the world bothered with lingering affection for an ex. This is a problem many women [and men] ignore or accept as normal. If you think it's natural for you to feel this way about someone long after they've moved on to another relationship, I want you to understand it's not. Grieve, and then let it go. If you can't let go, then that's the part that's not natural or normal. You don't have to live with persistent feelings that keep you in bondage to a person who left you.

WHAT TO EXPECT WHEN GOD PURGES THE HEART

"My dear friend (Sabrina), listen to what I'm about to tell you. Satan has demanded to come and sift you like wheat and test your faith. But I [Jesus] have prayed for you that you would stay faithful to me no matter what comes. Remember this: after you have turned back to me and have been restored, make it your life mission to strengthen the faith of your brothers." Luke 22:31-32 (TPT)

I purposely inserted by name in the scripture above as a reminder that I too was a radical believer like Peter, who Jesus was talking to in the verse. But even after years of knowing Christ, and loving him just as Peter did, my commitment to him was still lacking. Satan desired to sift me like wheat and test my faith. Now that I've turned back to Jesus and have been restored, it is my life's mission to strengthen the faith of my sisters. Today, I live my life for His glory.

-Sabrina

CHAPTER 2

THE EX FACTOR

Daughters of God, my sisters in the faith, I hear your cry for help. When you love someone, like an ex-boyfriend, ex-husband, ex-lover or a former relationship, and the relationship ends for whatever reason, there's a feeling of substantial loss. Some of you recovered quickly. Others of you, although it may have taken a few months to go through the grieving process and eventually move on, you did it. But then, there are others, like me, who shoved the emotions down because they were too hurtful to deal with at the time. The problem with shoving emotions down is that they don't stay down. Eventually, those emotions rise again and typically because you're having overwhelming thoughts about your ex that stir them up. Over time, this can become overwhelming and depressing.

I want you to know that God understands your loss and heartbreak. He can heal the hurt you feel and remove those overwhelming thoughts and emotions about your exes. Our God is full of compassion, mercy, and grace, and he knows about what you're going through. You don't have to hide or bury your feelings. God is here with a message for you that He will help you out of this situation.

I am without question the right person to talk with you about this issue. I identify with you, and I know what it's like to have something bothering you that is so intimate and private that you can't share with anyone else. I know all too well about the struggle of a lingering 'feeling of love' for someone that just won't go away even though you are married to someone else or that person is married to someone other than you. I'm glad you trust me enough to openly talk about what's bothering you. I can help you because God, my heavenly Father, helped me.

Although I'm not in the situation now, praise God Almighty for complete healing, deliverance, and restoration, I've been there. Don't be ashamed that your issue exists or that you haven't been able to break free from the loss of a man you once loved. I thought I was going crazy because 20 years had passed and yet I was still stuck in 1979, the year the relationship ended. I still had an attachment to that relationship.

When you talk about keeping your struggle a secret, this was a big one that troubled me for years because I was married. The first time I realized my problem was epic was on my actual wedding night. I never would have imagined that as my husband and I walked into our bridal suite at the Sheraton Hotel in downtown Atlanta, a ghost from my past would follow me into that elegant room.

Our suite was a wedding gift for us to share our first night as husband and wife. It was a sight to see; huge and beautifully decorated. When we walked into the suite we were wowed! We looked at each other and smiled, we were so happy that this day was the official beginning of our life together as Mr. and Mrs.

We walked around the room noticing the king-size bed decorated with rose petals, sparkling apple cider cooling in an ice bucket on display (the person who gave us the gift made arrangements to have it in our room before we arrived), and the enormous bathroom shower we both could fit in that was much larger than the bathroom in the apartment we would soon call home. After we explored our room for about 10 or 15 minutes, there was a knock at the door. Room service was delivering a large tray of fresh chocolate-covered strawberries, my favorite treat, and a chilled bottle of champagne the hotel gifted us. Real champagne. We were grinning from cheek-to-cheek. There we were 20 years old, grown and married, and about to drink champagne for the first time. At our wedding, we served punch. Isn't that funny? It cracks me up thinking about it today.

Drinking champagne was not the only thing we did for the first time that night. We were both virgins, and as soon as we finished all those chocolate-covered strawberries, we consummated our marriage. The moment we had been waiting for, right? My husband and I laughed because our experience wasn't like the soap opera romances I watched religiously on TV. But hey, we live and learn. I'm being facetious; we were a bit awkward but no complaints from either of us.

My husband went for a shower and I reached for the phone to call my mom to share the exciting news that I was no longer a virgin. She laughed and told me I was silly crazy. We both laughed. But, when I hung up the phone with mom the laughing stopped. And as I lay in bed a fleeting memory of my ex crossed my mind, and I wondered what it would have been like had he been there with me (as my husband) on my wedding night as I had always believed he would be the one. I thought I had put my feelings about him to sleep years ago, but nope, during that moment they crept up. Ugh!

By the time my husband stepped out of the shower and came back into the room with me, that fleeting thought was gone. Yay! I took my shower, we ate leftover food from our wedding, and then we snuggled up and talked all night long, reflecting on the excitement of our wedding day and enjoying the moment until we fell asleep. The next morning, we woke up and got dressed for church as usual. As far as I was concerned, that fleeting thought was gone forever.

But it wasn't.

If there is anyone who can understand you being overwhelmed by the memory of a man you once loved, I can. If there is anyone qualified to help you understand what's wrong and answer some questions you have, I can. I know why you're having these problems and God wants me to share my testimony with you so you'll know what to do and what not to do when He begins to purge your ex from your heart. His mission is for you to be free of this situation; he wants to give you peace and save you from everything in your past that is haunting you today.

But first, before we tackle the issue you're having, I have a few things I want to say to you because I don't want you to take any impulsive actions today that may backfire or wreak havoc later, either in your life or someone else's life. The following seven points of wisdom may sound a little harsh, but that's not my intention. I just don't want you to rashly do something you'll regret.

CHAPTER 3

7 POINTS OF WISDOM

1. Leave him alone

In 1999 my ex-boyfriend and I reconnected through phone calls. Although exciting and innocent in the beginning, it wasn't easy for me when the time came for us to stop talking and move on with our lives. After all the years that past, I didn't want to lose him again. Initially, I felt like I could handle talking with him and didn't foresee an issue. He was an ex, but he was also a friend, and I enjoyed talking with him just as I always did in the past.

Catching up with him allowed me to share the difficulty I experienced after the breakup. Finally, I could open up and have the heart to heart talk to say how I felt that I didn't express back then. In retrospect, honestly, I didn't need to do that. It wasn't wise of me, nor righteous of me, to get involved with him in any way.

If you feel like you want to talk with the man in your past my urgent advice to you - don't do that. Don't try to find him, don't talk with him under any circumstances, not even through friends you may have in common and run into at the mall one day. Don't inform him, by any means, that you love him or have feelings for him, and don't ever mention or entertain the thought of you wanting him back. What's going on with you emotionally or physically has nothing to do with him. Leave him alone! Even if he is reaching out to you and showing you that he cares about your feelings, leave him alone! What you are feeling is about you, not him. Leave him alone.

Since this is about you

- Don't create opportunities to talk with him.
- Don't respond to friends who may try to reconnect the two of you.
- Don't makeup reasons to visit him.
- Don't accept invitations from him to visit.
- Don't run to him about your problem as if he's still your friend or boyfriend.

Talking with him draws you to the relationship and gives false hope that you might get back together one day. It delays your healing, and you'll find yourself having to part from him again.

Don't be dependent upon him to meet your needs in any way; that's not healthy for you. He is not your source. Only God can meet your needs. God is your source, not your ex.

He's not your friend in the same way any longer, especially if he's married or in another relationship. Don't view him as a friend even if he's the best friend you've ever had. He's not your enemy either, at least I hope not, but don't view him as a friend that you 'need' is the point I'm making. You don't 'need' him; you need to release yourself from the thought of him. He's already released himself from you, especially if he is married or seeing someone else.

Don't **bother** him. Let me interject and list a few synonyms to explain the meaning of the word bother: worry, trouble, problem, or hassle. Here's a breakdown for the meaning of bother that I want you to apply to your situation … don't worry that man, don't trouble or cause trouble for that man, don't be a problem for that man, and don't hassle that man. Leave him alone! Further, we can also flip this statement and apply this message to you in this way… don't allow that man to worry you, don't let that man cause trouble for you, don't let him be a problem and hassle you. Leave him alone!

2. It's over; move forward

I don't mean to hurt your feelings, but when a man ends a relationship with you it's because he doesn't want to be in a relationship with you, and there isn't anything you can do to change his mind so don't try. Move forward. I don't

WHAT TO EXPECT WHEN GOD PURGES THE HEART

care how hard it is or how bad it hurts you, face it. Don't make-believe as if it didn't happen. This may be easier said than done but do it anyway.

As soon as someone ends a relationship with you, it's over. I want to do a plug-in again to drill this into your understanding. As soon as your ex-boyfriend, ex-husband, an ex-lover or anyone you've been in a relationship with, ends their relationship with you, it's over.

Many people may not agree with my next statement, but I will say it anyway … go dead silent and do not say a mumbling word in response to his decision to leave you other than you understand his choice and accept his decision to leave. That's it, now go silent with him. You're not silent out of anger or bitterness, that's not the reason. You are silent because there is nothing else that needs to be said or talked about. It's over.

If he wants to give you a why, listen if you feel obliged if you think it will help you move forward, but it's not necessary (I caution you against it, frankly). If his decision has already been made, then there is no reason to tell you why he has made the choice to leave you.

Hearing his reasoning will only hurt you more and make you want to prove him wrong or coerce him into staying with you. Don't do that. His reason why could create yet another emotion that's not good for you, and it's possible to be pacifying and not his true reason. It may be hurtful and painful and could tear down your self-esteem. You don't need that. Be pleasant but let him take his [why] with him when he walks away from you. If something is going wrong in a relationship, whatever the problem, it should be discussed before the announcement that the relationship has come to an end. With his decision being final already your only response is to move forward. If he is kind and caring and just wants to end the relationship and is letting you know, appreciate his honesty and move forward.

Now let's say he tried to talk with you before this final decision, but you refused to listen and acknowledge the issues and take the opportunity to resolve them, but instead, you ignored the issue. Still, at this point, your only choice is to move forward and don't beat yourself up about it. You can move forward.

Harping over why he made the decision will cause you to feel miserable, so don't harp. Wishing you would have communicated better or differently doesn't change the reality of the end. There isn't anything else you two need to say to each other unless you have children together and will come in contact with each other. Otherwise, don't share anything personal about yourself with him going forward, not even how you feel about the breakup. He is not the one you should talk to about that. You can't move forward if he stays in the picture in any way.

Why am I so stern about moving forward? Because ...

- You don't have time to waste staying connected to a relationship that's already over.
- That person is not the one for you; be okay with that.
- If you go back, you are agreeing to continue to experience heartbreak again and again. Don't do that.
- If you go back you are teaching the person you will accept being treated disrespectfully, devalued, and a beggar desperate for love. You are better than that. You are surrounded by love. Open your eyes to see the love in front of you.
- If you go back, you are setting yourself up to be used and discarded again later. Don't allow that to happen.
- If you go back, you are acting weak. You're not weak, God made you strong and courageous.
- Lastly, you have nothing to go back to. It's over.

3. This is about you

When someone no longer wants to be in a relationship with you, and that news leaves you struggling, literally paralyzed emotionally, then your struggle is about you and not the other person. Why haven't you been able to let the relationship go twenty years later? What does that say about you? Remember, it's over, so there isn't anything tangible for you to hold on to. It's over. You are no longer in a relationship.

WHAT TO EXPECT WHEN GOD PURGES THE HEART

Let me ask you a question. When you hear it's over, how does that make you feel? I want you to allow yourself to feel whatever that is, and then I want you to think about those feelings for a few minutes. Get a notebook, title the notebook Personal Prayer Points, and write down all of the feelings you just had into your private notebook. Put the notebook aside until a later time. I want to teach you how to express your feelings to God in prayer.

The feelings you wrote privately may be similar to the list below. Hearing it's over made me feel:

- Disappointed and anxious
- Hurt
- Abandoned
- Rejected
- Unloved
- Unworthy
- Lonely
- Like a failure
- Not good enough
- Like I want to change his mind
- Life is not worth living
- Like escaping the pain
- Like I did something wrong
- Like, no, it's not over

If you wrote anything from the list above, know that those feelings are expected and even typical when someone you care about no longer cares for you or doesn't care for you in the same way as before. I want you to know it's okay and I understand; God understands. We will pray about all those things you wrote down and more. You don't have to struggle with your feelings in silence. Learning to talk to Jesus and share your emotions with him in prayer is the best way to handle anything and everything, including getting over a breakup.

4. Stop talking to the wrong people about it. Pray, talk to God.

It's okay to spill your guts talking about how you feel, but you have to make sure you're talking to the right person who cares about you and can help you. Exes are never the right people to talk to about your feelings after the breakup. The person to talk to is not your best friend or your mama; it's God. I'm not saying don't ever talk to your best friend or mama, but in some cases can't nobody help you but God. Some pain can run so deep that it's beyond another human's ability to help. Let the first person you run to be God. Run to him as often as you need to during the day or night. Then, if your best friend and mama are praying people who will intercede for you before God and strengthen you with the Word of God, by all means, confide in them. Otherwise, there is no need to share with them either. What would be the point of talking to anyone about how you feel if they are not praying for you or strengthening you with encouraging words from the Bible. I do believe God has people he purposely connects us with to help us when we are in trouble, but they need to have the wisdom that comes from God to pour into you that propels you towards healing. Ultimately, he wants us to run to him for help first, so go into your bedroom, prayer closet, shower, car or wherever you have alone time, and you pour your heart out to Jesus Christ.

Sometimes people want to help and they may even care to some degree, but they have their problems, relationship issues, and worries. They have families, they work, and they're busy. Get somewhere quiet and pray to Jesus and tell him how you feel, how you are disappointed, how you love the person and how you miss them. Release your emotions in the presence of the Lord. Tell him you are hurting and ask him to heal your hurt. You will find comfort and strength with him. Jesus will draw close to you as you draw close to him. He's the one who can heal all of your hurts and resolve all of your issues, including your feelings after a breakup. Jesus created you, and so he knows you better than anybody. He knows you better than you know yourself.

You may wonder if I know all of this then why did I struggle silently for so long? That's a good question. The answer is complex with not just one answer, but many. I struggled because I was in denial. I struggled because I didn't know how to adequately express my feelings to anyone – not to him, not to my best friend, not to my mom, and not to God. I was so overwhelmed with emotions that it became too much for me. The only way I knew to handle it was to put my emotions to sleep. Still, I hoped that one day he would come back. That was false hope. He never came back.

Twenty years after the breakup I started praying about my feelings. They were still alive, just dormant. I don't want you to wake up twenty years from now praying about something that God can handle and resolve for you today, in this season. Talk to God now, tell him everything, and make sure you ask him to remove all false hope, help you to accept the truth, invite him into your emotions to settle you and heal you. Through prayer, you will learn that he will do what you can't do. He will purge it out of you.

5. Give your heart to Jesus Christ and love him fully

If you haven't already accepted Jesus Christ as your Lord and Savior, do it now. Open your heart to him. God wants us to love others and he wants us to experience being in love, but he doesn't want us to love others more than we love him. I encourage you to love God more.

When you love someone more than you love God it gets in the way of true worship because your heart is not fully yielded to him. When you are not yielded to him, you will serve and obey the person you love the most. Who is more deserving of your love above Jesus Christ? Who else is worthy to give you eternal life? The kind of love Jesus has for you is immeasurable, and it will never change and never fade away.

Still, if you decide you don't want to love him anymore, even though it may grieve his heart, even Jesus will have to let you go. Jesus will move forward. He cannot force you to love him just as you cannot force someone to love you.

I have a question. If you are quick to give your heart fully to a man who abuses you verbally and emotionally, uses your body for his good pleasure, take all that you have to offer and leaves you feeling empty and alone, doesn't spend any quality time with you or demonstrate any real love towards you, then why are you giving him your whole heart and not giving your whole heart to Jesus Christ?

You put a man on a pedestal and worship everything about him and kick Jesus to the curb, but it is Jesus who gave his all for you. Jesus is the one who died for you so you wouldn't suffer for your sins. Why persist with a counterfeit, fantasy-type love when you can have true love from Jesus whose personality and character is love. Beloved, Jesus is love. Read 1 John 4:8.

Open your heart, invite Jesus in, pursue him and you will learn to love him. He will teach you how to love him. Those of us who have already given our heart to Jesus, yet still holding on to the relationships in our past, let's give Jesus (ALL) of our heart, and not just a small portion. Let's turn our focus and energy back to God, our first love.

6. You don't have time to waste

Today is the time for you to make quality life decisions and choices that enhance your life. Decide to take responsibility for your well-being and emotional health. Choose to be mature and think about what you want from this life God has given you. If you want to be in a relationship, are you willing to trust God's timing for that relationship to occur and develop? Are you willing to date in a way that pleases God? Do you feel like something is missing if you're not in a relationship and, if you do, why is that? If you want a husband, act like it and don't waste time spending time with a man just because he's a man and you want him. And if you already have a husband, you don't have time to waste rehearsing the time you spent with an ex. Time is valuable, don't waste it.

If you've dated someone for a year or more and it didn't result in marriage at the end, you've wasted a year or more of your time. It doesn't mean you don't have good memories with the person, at least in your mind, but now you want to date again and hope for the best in your next relationship. This pattern cannot continue. You've got to make changes in your thinking and behavior before you consider involving yourself in another relationship.

7. Set standards for dating (single ladies)

You should have standards for dating. If you don't, you'll be tossed around in multiple pointless relationships and that's not good. If you don't have standards, don't date because you're not ready to date. You will go for anything and anybody. No standards, no dating. You will be played with like a toy and no man will take you seriously.

Here's an example of having standards:

1. No sex (fornicating) before marriage. Don't just talk it, mean it.
2. No tolerance for being disrespected.
3. Quality time with you and your immediate family is a must.
4. Someone who genuinely cares for you.
5. You want someone who enjoys church, prayer, praise, and worship.
6. No online dating.

Here's an example of compromising your standards:

1. Sex (fornicating) after three (3) dates or three (3) months. He knew you would.
2. He yells at you and makes you feel sad and hurt all the time, yet you continue to spend time with him and talk with him. Teaching him that his behavior is acceptable.
3. He makes excuses not to visit you or attend any of your family social events, and you accept it. Of course, you attend all of his events when (or if) he chooses to include you.
4. You feel you're last on his list of important people. He disappoints you, yet you continue seeing him.
5. He doesn't have a relationship with God and doesn't attend church, yet you continue to date unequally yoked.

6. Online dating is for the hookup. That's all it is, a new way to hookup, but that's your source to 'find' you somebody.

Here's an example of sticking with your standards:

1. No sex (fornicating) before marriage even if it means losing the relationship.
2. Any sign of disrespect towards you and all communication ends immediately.
3. He's not invested in you so you don't waste your time dealing with him.
4. As soon as you feel unimportant, and you have evidence to prove it and it's not your imagination or misunderstanding, don't waste your time with this person.
5. You immediately know he's not the one for you based on your standards so you don't waste your time.
6. No online dating even if all of your friends are doing it. It's a no for you, even if the whole world is doing it. Meet people so you can observe them and know who they are, and that can't happen online.

The list for setting standards can be very long and extensive. When you set your standards do not compromise them and don't feel compelled to talk about them. Here's what I mean:

As you determine your standards know that action speaks louder than words. At the beginning of a relationship don't talk too much. Be who you are and it will become obvious and clear to the other person who you are. If you are consistently your genuine self, he will know who you are and respond appropriately. If you are a true Christian in your heart, he will know it. If you talk religion but have no real relationship with Jesus Christ, he will know it immediately or very soon. He will play the religious talk game with you, but ultimately he will know you're just like everybody else and not special. Full of talk. Carry yourself like a lady and avoid nonsense talk that has no substance. Talk about a book you're reading and how it's inspiring you to be a better person, self-development. Talk about a class you're taking to improve your skills, inquire about his goals and plans for his own life. Have fun. Learn about his family, hobbies, interesting memories he has to share. Go places, but do not end up at his house and in his bed. You know why? Because you have standards and you are a woman of wisdom. You have standards!

WHAT TO EXPECT WHEN GOD PURGES THE HEART

Pray

Heavenly Father, I declare and decree that your daughters will not call, follow after, or chase no man or human, but we turn our hearts to call on you, follow after you, chase after you. For you alone are worthy of our devotion. You alone are worthy of our praise. Our hearts, minds, emotions, and attention are yours. Your daughters are not idol stalkers. Your daughters are women in love with you and the persistent pursuit of you only. We observe your ways and act just like you, our Father. Your daughters constantly think of you, and it is you we desire to fellowship with and bask in your presence. We lack nothing, because we have you, the Almighty looking out for our best interest. We, your daughters, take back our focus from the men the enemy used to steal our hearts, kill our dreams, and destroy us emotionally. It wasn't the men, it was the devil using them and it was us placing them above you. We repent! This ends today. We are no longer distracted by fantasies, daydreams, nightdreams, and unfulfilled longings. That is not our portion. You have husbands in mind for us, and we will love our husbands with the love of Jesus that flows through us to them. We are daughters of the Most High God. We are princesses and queens. We are the apple of your eye. We are loved and adored by you. We say goodbye to our exes (ex-boyfriends, ex-husbands, former relationships and ex-lovers). Lord, bless them. We are not bitter, we are not angry, we are free in our souls and we release them in the name of Jesus. And Lord, we thank you that no one is above you, not today, tomorrow or in the future. Amen.

WHAT TO EXPECT WHEN GOD PURGES THE HEART?

TRUTH

CHAPTER 4

THE TRUTH IS THE LIGHT

Let's think about your struggle realistically. If the man you love so much had equal love for you, he would be with you. If the man I felt I loved so much had equal love for me, he would be with me. The truth is you would be a couple if he equally wanted to be with you. Let's take a pause and allow that statement to resonate.

I don't know why that thought never crossed my mind all the years I spent being crazy in love and not able to move forward. He was special to me, but it never dawned on me that I wasn't special to him in the same way. Duh! So, hear me in love … you're not special to this guy you think you want to reach back to get. You're not the significant other if you're the one reaching back. You're not the significant other if he's not in your present willingly. Guess what, you're still breathing and you're still significant to those God has designed for your life. Let's take another pause and allow that statement to resonate. Amen.

Because of my experience, I'm compelled to tell you to quickly accept the truth. When you acknowledge the relationship is over and you accept that truth, you then make tremendous progress and you'll be just fine. Trust me. The only reason you're struggling with the breakup is that you refuse to accept it's over, and no one else can help you do that. Decide to accept it. It's not hard; stop telling yourself it's too hard. It's not. I did it kicking and screaming, but I did it. We all have to come to acceptance before we can put the past behind us.

How do you decide to accept that it's over? Well, look around and tell me who do you see in your everyday life? Is he there? No, he's not. Is he calling you to take you out on a date? Is he making plans to be with you at all? Are you home alone? Does he wish you a happy birthday? Does he come to see you at Christmas (or any holiday)? Does he stop by to visit you for no other reason than the fact that he just wants to see you, enjoy your company, and wants to spend time with you? He doesn't, does he? Then that truth is what makes your decision easy to make.

Let's just say, for the sake of an example, that he comes to visit you or asks to take you out on a date. After the date is over do you feel it was more about him and his needs being met and that the date had absolutely nothing to do with him enjoying you as a person? You are the only person who can answer this question. Do you feel empty after you spend time with him? Again, you are the only person who can answer this question. If a person can walk out of your life without looking back, pay attention to that and love yourself enough to see it for what it is and make a decision to accept it's over. Stop dealing with a nothing relationship. I don't care if he was your boyfriend, husband or whoever, once he leaves, stop dealing with a nothing relationship. Be real about what you see, hear, feel regarding this person and accept that reality. That's how you decide that it's over.

The truth is you can let the person go. Yes, you can! People do this every day and so can you. If you feel like you can't let go, that feeling is wrong. It's based on a lie and it's a trick being played on your mind. I don't care if you have to say it aloud 100 times a day, you say it ... (I can let him go, I can let him go, I can let him go). You say it as many times as necessary. Every time you feel like you can't, you respond with yes, I can. And no matter how you feel (good, bad, happy, or sad) don't bother that man.

When a person doesn't love you that doesn't mean you're not worthy of love. It only means he wasn't the right person for you; that's all it means and nothing more. Don't try to figure it out and allow your mind to create problems about your value and worth, which will throw you into a greater struggle of despair. He doesn't love you and that doesn't make him a bad person. My mama told me that. She was right, he wasn't a bad person. He's a great person, but he wasn't the god I made him out to be. The guy your heart is panting for is not God either. At this point, he's no longer a topic of our conversation. I want to make sure we focus on you and what's happening with your emotions.

Pray

Heavenly Father,
Thank you for teaching us how to distinguish between what is true and what is a lie. We have eyes to see the truth. We have ears to hear the truth. We have the discernment needed to acknowledge the truth. We are not twisted romantically; we are wise, honorable, respectable daughters. We carry ourselves well, and we pay attention to your promptings and leadings in who we should befriend, date, and marry. We will to distance ourselves and walk away from those who you didn't send. We are emotionally fit and stable because you designed us that way. We have the mind of Christ and reject any way of thinking and behaving that is contrary to who you created us to be. We walk in righteousness and holiness. We live and breathe and enjoy this life that you gave us. We are your daughters and that alone makes us special, valuable and worthy of the best that you have for us. In Jesus' name, we pray. Amen.

CHAPTER 5

IDENTIFYING THE PROBLEM RESOLVING THE ISSUE

Now, let's tackle the real issues that concern you. The idea, thoughts or hope of rekindling a relationship with an ex is part of the problem, but not the root of the problem. They produce romantic desires, sexual fantasies, and impure thoughts that hide behind a wrong belief. The true problem is your belief system that is influencing your heart. Your misguided beliefs about the ex-boyfriend, ex-husband, ex-lover or former relationship must be purged from your heart.

Your wrong beliefs coupled with the fact that you're married (or your ex is married), make resolving and correcting this issue an urgent matter.

Whew! You've got yourself a big problem. But, be encouraged, it's not too big for God to solve. As long as you're ready to confront these problems head-on and be a hundred percent transparent, then we can begin to stop these emotions once and for all. You've been carrying an unrelenting burden, a very serious burden, in secret form, but we're going to no longer keep it a secret. We are going to expose it all in prayer.

First, I want to open your eyes so you can see what's wrong. It's time for you to be free of this secret so you can enjoy your life. Again, I struggled likewise and felt defeated because of my all-consuming thoughts. I want you to know that deception is at the root of your beliefs, and the Devil is downloading the deception into your mind. He targets the mind to get a stronghold into your life. I was deceived in my belief system at one point, and God delivered me from the lie I believed. He will deliver you too. The following are some of the problems you're facing that you might not realize.

Problem 1

Satan is tempting you. Being tempted is the desire to engage in short-term urges for enjoyment or pleasure. It is the inclination to sin. Temptation happens when you are being persuaded or provoked into committing an act, by manipulation or otherwise of curiosity, desire or fear of loss. (Wikipedia)

In other words, the enemy is persuading you that no other man can take the place of your ex, or he's making you think that you will be happier with this one person in your life. There is something about the person you're consumed with that you like or want. I don't know if it's the way he looks, talk, walk or smile, but whatever it is you desire him for yourself and the devil knows it. If he can get you to believe you should be with this person and lures you with romantic urges, fantasies, and thoughts, and you go after this person, then he would have successfully tempted you into sin. When you pursue this person and pulls him into your deception, then the enemy would have successfully tempted both of you into sin.

Satan is tricky and a master deceiver. He works all avenues to bring his plan of destruction into your life. He may create the thoughts in you and have you pursue your ex, or he may create thoughts in your ex and send him to pursue you knowing you've never gotten over the relationship in the first place and are just waiting for an opportunity to get back with him. The enemy may time it so that you both are pursuing each other. Who knows? The point is, take note and be watchful, you may not be the one doing the pursuing. Either way, he is working behind the scenes.

The desire to regain something you've lost and the belief that no one else can take this person's place in your heart will eventually get the best of you and overtake you if you allow it to linger without proactively resisting the enemy. You believe you should be with this other person, but you're wrong. Realize that what's in your heart, what you're thinking and feeling, is wrong and that your belief is wrong.

WHAT TO EXPECT WHEN GOD PURGES THE HEART

Temptations will continue as long as this person remains your weakness and you embrace your desire for him. With this mindset, you are giving him a legal right to tempt you. He is going to use this desire to destroy you if you continue to indulge in his promptings instead of listening to the voice of God. No matter how often you are tempted, and to what degree you're tempted, it's still your responsibility to obey God. If you engage in a relationship with this person to satisfy the desire you have for him, or if you connect with him in any way, you will regret it. You don't realize this now because it feels like love, but as soon as you complete the act of lust (not love) and give in to the temptation, you will immediately know that you don't love this person. Then, guilt and shame will torture you and you'll wish it never happened.

Therefore, every time you have thoughts of calling him or wanting to be with him I want you to know that the enemy is luring you. Don't carry on a conversation with the enemy by allowing those thoughts to remain unchecked. He's making you think you missed out on something good and now you want to reach back to get it. It's an illusion and a big mistake, so don't do it. Remember, the enemy has captured your thoughts to focus on what you feel you lost or wanted. His purpose is to entice you to sin and live a life that displeases God.

I want you to know that just because he is tempting you it doesn't mean you have to do what he says. He cannot make you or force you to do anything. Being tempted is not a sin. When you give in to the temptation by doing what the enemy is luring you to do, which is to satisfy your desire for this guy, then the temptation turns into sin. Remember, you don't have to do anything the enemy wants you to do by allowing your feelings to get the best of you. Resist him.

Resolution 1

How do you resist temptation? Let's look at scriptures to get the answer. James 4:7 says to give yourself completely to God. Stand against the devil, and the devil will run from you. When you stand against the devil you depend on scriptures from the word of God and follow them, which means to obey them. You will have to resist the enemy's temptations over and over again to prove to him that you will obey God no matter what. Remember scriptures. You cannot fight against temptation on your own, you need to know the mind of Christ concerning the thing the enemy is luring you towards. Resisting temptation develops your character as a Christian, and it also lets you know where you stand in your relationship with Christ. It answers the question of your commitment to Jesus. Are you committed to Jesus? It's a personal question that only you can answer.

When you face temptation consider the outcome of your actions if you decide to engage. Ask yourself these questions taken from the Life Application Study Bible; they will help you make the right choice:

- Does it help my witness for Christ?
- Does it help others to know Christ?
- Is it contrary to scripture, causing me to sin?
- Am I thinking only of myself, or do I truly care about the other person?
- Am I acting lovingly or selfishly?
- Does it glorify God?
- Will it cause someone else to sin?

By the time you process these questions, you should be able to make the right decision and escape temptations.

Matthew 26:41 says to watch and pray so that you will not fall into temptation. Don't take your thoughts and feelings lightly. Watch over your thoughts and feelings, pay attention, and pray about them so that you will not fall into temptation. Don't keep them a secret from God. Take action, be proactive, and don't sleep on this or be lazy about praying. Pray always.

In fact, with every temptation, God provides a way of escape. God is faithful. 1 Corinthians 10:13 says the only temptation that has come to you is that which is common to all of us. But you can trust God, who will not permit you to be tempted more than you can stand. But when you are tempted, he will also give you a way to escape so that you will be able to stand it. Don't be surprised if the person you're attracted to rejects you. That's God providing a way of escape for you. Walk away and be thankful for the escape. Some women may not have been so fortunate to escape.

Problem 2

You're dealing with addiction or addictive personality. Synonyms for addiction are obsession, habit, infatuation, compulsion, and dependence. When applying this meaning to your situation, you are obsessed or leaning towards an obsession for your ex. You have formed a compulsive habit of thinking about him and is infatuated with him specifically. You are dependent upon him, and that's why the idea or thought of him continues to preoccupy and intrude on your mind.

Whenever you are fixated with one person (or more) and have recurring thoughts that have you seeking the person out, the enemy is at work in your life. So far, you have been unsuccessful fighting against this addiction, especially if this has been ongoing in your life even during your marriage. You are in spiritual warfare and wrestling with the enemy and all of his wicked buddies and imps. Right now, you're getting beat up by these enemies and you're not even trying to fight back. Arm yourself with the word of God and take your mind back. You will be victorious if you cooperate with the word of God. Are you willing to fight for your freedom?

Resolution 2

Addictions form over time and grow to out of control behavior. Get rid of this addiction before it destroys you and others. If you are a strong-willed person determined to get what you want and refuse to take no for an answer, your strong-will is a problem and the enemy will use it to his advantage.

Create a visual, for example. See yourself loading all of your thoughts and desires for your ex and putting them into a huge barrel that you seal shut and can never reopen. You've got to be willing to push that barrel over a cliff down into a vast sea and watch it sink into the depths of the sea until it is no longer visible. Then, you've got to be willing to turn around and walk away, and never look back. You've got to be willing to let go of the addiction, wicked thoughts, and desires… you've got to want to drive the negatives out of your life.

An addict will seal the barrel shut and push it to the edge of the cliff but will not have the will power to push the barrel over the cliff. Instead, an addict will find a tool to unseal the barrel and take everything out again unwilling to let go. Or, an addict will have the will power to push the barrel over but will dive into the sea afterward to attempt to recover it; unwilling to let it go.

Now, you can do this visual in your mind, but becoming free from addictions is not that easy. It's going to take work and you'll have to be consistent, honest and willing to give up your mindset regarding your ex. You cannot be strong-willed. Release your will in exchange for God's will. Are you willing to release those thoughts and desires (by placing them in a barrel and turning your back on them)? Do you want to give them up (or push them over a cliff into the sea)? Or, will you go back to the addiction because it's too hard to let go? People addicts must do the same thing to get clean as drug addicts and alcohol addicts; you've got to want to give up your drug of choice. Exercise self-control and make a decision to choose God instead of the addiction; choose God over the ex, and instead of pursuing the ex, pursue God.

Galatians 5:22 describes self-control as a fruit of the Spirit. It's a character trait of Jesus Christ, which is what you want. Reconnect with Jesus and allow the Holy Spirit to produce self-control in your life. Ask him to do it. A lack of self-control plus addictions, on the other hand, will cause you to behave contradictory to the life of a Christian. Don't allow addictions or an addictive personality to produce bad fruit in your life. Instead, crucify your flesh with its passions and desires. You cannot do this on your own. Ask God in prayer to crucify (kill) your passions and desires and remove all addictions that are trying to rule you. In prayer, openly renounce any addiction to this person (and say the person's name).

Problem 3

Satan is oppressing you. The enemy's entire history has been to persecute and harass Christians, and all of humanity. He is a cruel and forever enemy of yours and mine. For him to oppress you, he has to influence some area in your life. With you and the thoughts you're battling, the enemy is using that influence to

WHAT TO EXPECT WHEN GOD PURGES THE HEART

weigh you down and put you under so much pressure that you will eventually lose your way and do anything for relief. He dominates and controls your beliefs about your ex, and that's why he's using his power and influence to crush your spirit. He wants you to think that the only way to get relief and escape the oppression is to get the guy.

Do you have an urge to reach out to the ex on social media? Do you feel pressure to contact your ex in any way? That's the Enemy urging and pressuring you. The enemy is turning up the heat on you. When the pressure is that heavy and you're being attacked day and night, the enemy has something brewing that will bring destruction. He's stirring the pot, so to speak. You won't be able to see the big picture but when you submit to the pressure and act according to his plans and schemes, an explosion will occur. Trouble will occur.

You see, you're just part of the equation. Your ex is the other part of the equation. You both have lives that involve other people. You don't know what's been going on in his life before you and he reconnected. If he's married, you don't know what he and his wife have been through or what they are going through. Things may be going well for them, their storm may be over, but the enemy will stir up yet another storm (YOU) to interrupt their lives and destroy their relationship and family. You've got to realize the enemy works on both sides of the fence. If he's harassing and attacking you with extreme intensity, you'd better believe it's for a reason. He's attacking them too, yet again, but this time he's using you to work his plan. Don't allow it. You have access to the Heavenly Father, and through him, you have victory if you obey him.

You've got to realize this as well, when you grow as a Christian and you're impacting the Kingdom of Heaven, leading people to accept Jesus Christ as Lord and Savior, the enemy will come after you. He has to try to stop you! And, if he has a stronghold in your life that's been dormant from childhood like he had in my life, he will manipulate and stir up that stronghold to stop your witness for Jesus. But know this, your enemy has no power over you. He is a defeated foe. Your strength and power source is Jesus Christ, and it is through Jesus you overcome all attacks against you.

Resolution 3

Ask God to reveal the truth behind the desires you have, and the truth about all influences the enemy has in your life. Believe what God says, and then ask him to deliver you from all wrong belief systems, repent of all sins, and the enemy cannot oppress you any longer. Oppression is all about persecution and harassment. All of that will go away and stop when you repent and yield to the Holy Spirit.

Confess your desire to God and turn away from it. It is what it is, so tackle this problem with honesty. If you desire this man, then telling God about it is the truth, and if you want to overcome this temptation and oppression, and be released from the addiction, ask God to purge you. Let God know you don't want to sin against him and that you need the help of the Holy Spirit to make a way of escape for you. Then, get in the word of God and search this out with scripture. Meditate on scriptures day and night. If you pray and mean it, and consistently invite God into this situation, he will rescue you from the enemy's plans and schemes. You cannot afford to be ignorant of the enemy's sinister schemes. The Bible has all the information you need, and the Holy Spirit will teach, advocate and help you through this situation.

Jesus is the resolution for all of our problems. Luke 4:18 tells us that he came to set the oppressed free. He doesn't want you secretly desiring your ex or anyone. He doesn't want you obsessed and yielding to temptation. He wants you saved and free. Jesus will tell you what happened in your life that gave the enemy the right to oppress you. Ask him to tell you and he will.

On the other hand, if you are a wayward Christian and rebelling against God through disobedience, he will allow the enemy to oppress you, but that would only be to get you to turn from sin and restore your relationship with him. He will allow it to bring you back into alignment with his will. Don't rebel against God.

Pray

Heavenly Father,

You are the author and finisher of our faith. You are the answer to every problem, the resolution to every conflict. We do not rebel against you for you are our protector and shield. Lead us away from temptation and deliver us from evil.

Hide us with your strong and mighty hand, and protect us against harm, danger, and the Devil. Purge our minds and remove all wrong beliefs from the enemy. Do not allow anything to destroy our witness for you, do not allow us to sin. We give you the authority to rule and reign in our life so that we can be the example that others need to see to know that you live through us.

We choose to cooperate with you by obeying your word. We ask for a heart to think of others more than we think of ourselves, and to think of you and what brings you honor and glory. In Jesus' name, we pray. Amen.

CHAPTER 6

RELATIONSHIPS WORK BEST WHEN GOD ESTABLISHES THEM HIS WAY

As a believer, you want God's approval of your relationships. It matters to him who you are connected with, including dating and marriage. God says do not be unequally yoked together with an unbeliever. Yet, we date and marry non-Christians all the time. We compromise and ignore what God says when we meet someone we're attracted to, right? All the person has to say is he believes in a higher power and we take that and run with it. We get involved in relationships without seeking God first, and then when the relationship fails and we find ourselves in trouble, we run to God hurting. He will help us and heal us, of course, but we can avoid the hardship if we just stay in his will when dating. He knows you and the plans he has for you, and some people just don't fit within those plans. You may not fit the plans he has for them either. Be okay with the relationships that God establishes for you and let him have his way. Give up control and trying to make people be apart of your life. Trust God's way.

The relationships established by God are purposed to bring joy into your life. First and foremost the relationship with Jesus Christ, our Lord, should be satisfying. Let your devotion, focus, and commitment be directed towards him. Don't be so engaged in satisfying your fleshly desires and wants for a relationship that you miss being married (united) to God first. You are his bride, remember that.

When you are married, daughters, one way that God works to bring you happiness is through the husband he provides for you. View your husband as a gift from God and know with certainty that you were made suitable for him. Be content with what you have. If you can't see this, it is because of the strong illusions the enemy is sending you about someone else, and that illusion is blocking your view. (Note: It's the illusion that is blocking your view, not the person you are fascinated with). Get rid of the illusion and the fascination disappears too.

A fantasy relationship is the work of the enemy. Everything that comes from him is false. That's how he defeats Christians and non-Christians alike, by making us think the thoughts we have are our own. They are not! Those thoughts are mere distractions. In Philippians 4:8 we're advised to think about the things that are good and worthy of praise. Think about the things that are true, honorable, right, pure, beautiful, and respectable.

Trust me, what you are dealing with has nothing to do with your former relationship. Instead, it has everything to do with thoughts from the enemy meant to destroy. Right now, he is targeting your relationship with Jesus and distracting you; he is tugging against your union with your husband, he's not happy you have been saved from eternal destruction through salvation and your faith in Jesus, he wants to ruin your testimony and have you walk away from eternal life with Christ. He wants to lure you away to someone who will not love you the way your husband loves you. The devil wants you in a bad, unhealthy relationship with a man who doesn't know God, your God, and won't know how to love you the way you deserve. Only someone who knows the heart of God concerning you can love you the way God wants his daughter to be loved.

I can tell the world that all I have ever received from my husband is love, consistent love. He was created to love me God's way. I have an incredible love story despite my trials and I attribute the success of our marriage to the Lordship of Jesus and our ultimate commitment to him.

When you don't take heed to God's precautions, you will live with the regrets of betraying Jesus and your husband all for naught. You will be miserable. The

WHAT TO EXPECT WHEN GOD PURGES THE HEART

man you think you love will never commit to you. A man who loves you will not have let you marry another man without first letting you know that he loves you and asks for you to marry him. If he didn't ask you to marry him, it means he doesn't want you as his wife. If he didn't find a way to let you know he loves you BEFORE you married someone else or he married someone else, it's because he doesn't love you. You should be okay with that and trust God for your spouse (the one you have). Men marry women they love. Your husband loves you and married you. Rest in that and let old relationships die.

As a married woman be concerned about how to please your husband. Allow God to transform your mind in favor of your husband. Now that God has healed and delivered me from the lies I believed, it's amazing how sweet it is to love my husband fully in the way he deserves. He's precious. I want you to focus on the blessing of what you have and not the distraction of what you feel like you lost. The truth is you gained. Your husband is a benefit and asset to your life. Your husband is married to you and if he is a true man of God, he is concerned about how to please you. Anything that draws you away from each other is a sin trap. Anything that draws you away from God is a sin trap.

CHAPTER 7

THE SIN TRAP

Your word I have treasured and *stored in my heart, that I may not sin against You.*
Psalm 119:11 (AMP)

Adultery. Adultery is willful sexual intercourse between a married person and someone other than the lawful spouse.

You are married and that's the first thing you need to keep in mind. As a married woman, when you think about another man sexually or romantically you are actively committing adultery because the other man is in your heart. Adultery doesn't begin when you have sex with a person you're not married to, it begins the moment that person is in your heart. It starts with the desire to be intimate with this person, even if that intimate desire is your secret and no one else knows. Even if you haven't acted on the feelings and the person you desire has no idea you feel that way, you are still guilty of adultery from God's perspective. In essence, you are cheating on your husband. You are unfaithful and emotionally unavailable to your legal spouse. You are also in an illegal, ungodly, sinful relationship. You don't want that in your life.

Further, if you were once married to someone but are now divorced from them and you are married to another man, it's still adultery if you entertain the memory of sexual intimacy with your first husband. It's still a sin. Break this sin cycle. The sin of adultery will cause you to end up in hell if you don't repent. Hear me in love. If you were to die today without sincerely repenting of adultery, you will not go to heaven. That's why I implore you not to bother that man in any form (even in your secret thoughts). If your ex-husband, ex-boyfriend, an ex-lover or any former relationship partner pursues you while they or married or you are married, flee! In your case, don't you be the one pursuing him either. Don't entertain the flattery (even if you think it's sincere flattery). It's a sin trap.

Do you realize that if you are desiring a man (bothering him) in your thoughts and he is married, you are not only committing adultery, but you are also guilty of coveting? He's another woman's husband. You are wrongfully desiring what belongs to her. When you think of him realize your real motive is to steal him away, the true desire of your heart, and that's a problem. One sin leads to other sins and they all (all the sin) keep you in bondage and in danger of being lost forever in sin if you don't seek Jesus for forgiveness. Confess it, repent of it and turn away from each sin.

Take a look at the following scriptures. Memorize them. Use them as your guideline for life.

1. Exodus 20:14 – Do not commit adultery.

2. Matthew 5:27 – If you look at a woman (or man) lustfully, you've already committed adultery with her (him) in your heart.

3. Hebrews 13:4 – Marriage should be honored by all, and the marriage bed kept pure, for God will judge the adulterer and all the sexually immoral.

4. 1 Corinthians 6:9 – Adulterers will not enter God's kingdom, Heaven.

5. Deuteronomy 5:21 – Do not covet or desire your neighbor's stuff (I added the word stuff); it means don't want anything that belongs to your neighbor (or any other person).

When you repent (remorsefully repent by turning away from adultery), the blood of Jesus washes away and covers the adultery and makes you clean from the sin stain and guilt it leads behind. So, in your prayer closet or wherever you are, confess and admit that you are guilty of adultery and covetousness and any other sins that fit this scenario (like stealing) and ask for forgiveness. You are

WHAT TO EXPECT WHEN GOD PURGES THE HEART

100% forgiven when you repent and stop entertaining and acting out on the thoughts of this other man. Those thoughts are not worth you spending eternity in a burning hell. Get rid of them! Use the memory verses you just learned and pray those scriptures every day until your heart is changed and your thoughts align with them. Thoughts about another man are not worth the time you could be spending worshiping God and enjoying your family. Don't miss heaven because you enjoy the thoughts in your head. I'm teaching you to fight against them in the name of Jesus. If any thoughts are causing friction between you and Jesus, they've got to go. Your relationship with God is uncompromisable so don't compromise. Adultery must go now!

Idolatry. Idolatry is the worship of a physical object as a god. It's an excessive attachment or devotion to something.

Idolaters are people who worship people or things as gods. That's you in the situation you're in right now with the ex-boyfriend, ex-husband, ex-lover or former relationship that you want back so badly. You esteem them so highly that you refuse to let them go. This stops today.

When a person becomes a symbol of pleasure for you in some way, a symbol of reverence, a hero, or an image in your mind that you highly adore, that means you are in idolatry. When the person means more to you than God, that's an idol. When you profess to worship the ground a man walks on and will do anything to please him, and you mean it, he's an idol in your heart. Going forward, don't ever let those words come out of your mouth, that you worship the ground any human being walks on. Don't allow that phrase to flow out of your mouth with so much pride; it's not cute. No human being deserves that kind of worship and allegiance. God is not pleased; he calls people who worship idols corrupt, and idolatry makes him angry. Get rid of anything or anybody in your heart (ex-boyfriend, ex-husband, etc.) that is taking God's place.

I get it because I did it. Sometimes we place people on pedestals without realizing it. But, he's just a man. He's a human being. It took a close friend of mine to tell me that this guy was just a man. That statement shook me a bit. Because in my mind, I saw him BIGGER than that and much more important than any other man. When she said that to me something clicked in my brain. Wow! It helped me to see clearly that I had a problem. Let me ask you a question. In what way do you view your ex, as a man or human being or do you see him as all that and a bag of chips? Will you do anything to get him back? Will you wait for him forever in hopes he'll come back to you? Do you measure every nice guy you meet in comparison to him?

God alone deserves your worship, honor, and respect in that way. Learn how to love a person without the element of bowing down to them in worship. To be clear, I want you to fully understand the definition of an idol and know that it's a false god. When you think you can't survive without this person in your life, or you feel you are nobody without them, you've idolized them. When you're willing to sin to keep them, instead of repenting and releasing them, you've chosen them above God.

When the Holy Spirit revealed to me that I was in idolatry I was shocked. I thought I was in love, and that's how the enemy tricked me. The Holy Spirit brought back to my memory the times as a young girl, I would wait for what seemed like hours on my grandmother's enclosed front porch, staring out of the window anticipating the object of my affection to walk down the street, pass her house going to the store or where ever, and then I would wait for him to come back up the street and pass her house again going home. He lived on the same street as my grandmother, up and over the hill. I remember this so vividly. Who knew idolatry was being formed in my heart during those impressive years of my life? The seeds were planted before I had any idea what the word idolatry meant or what obsessive behavior looked like.

Some people may describe it as an innocent childhood crush. It was that, but more extreme in my case. And, it was God who, during my adult years, explained the extreme factor when I asked him to help me understand the strong affection. God took me back in time, and he revealed the what, when, where, why and how the 'extreme' attachment was created. When you read my testimony in Part III of this book you'll understand.

The point I'm emphasizing, daughters of God, is for you to be careful and watchful to not idolize men as gods. Stop calling men your King. He's not your King, Jesus is your King. I understand if you're married and you respectfully refer to your husband as king with a lower k, especially if he's treating you like a queen, taking care of his household (wife and children), and loving you like Christ loves the church. But if you're not married, don't do that. It's popular nowadays for women to say, I'm waiting for my King, meaning they're waiting for God to bring them a husband. How about acknowledging God as your One and only King and asking God for a husband. Don't put your husband on the pedestal of a King to be worshipped. Just love, honor and respect your husband. He's the head of household, the leader in the home, but he's not a royal King.

Frankly, I recommend avoiding the title altogether. We take things a little too far, in my opinion, and it runs too close to idolatry. When you use that term as a sentimental and respectful title of honor and respect for your spouse, I get it. But, I tread very lightly on it because of the propensity I have to create and worship idols of the people I love. For me, the Lord is my King, with a capital K. To my husband, I extend other pet names to honor him respectfully, just not King or king. The title of 'husband' has a respectable ring to it all by itself.

Take a look at the following scriptures. Memorize them. Use them as a guideline for life.

1. Exodus 20:3 – I will put no other gods before You.
2. 1 John 5:21 - I will keep myself from idols.
3. Ezekiel 44:10 - Let me not go astray after any idol.
4. Ezekiel 36:25 – cleanse me from all idols.

Romantic Fantasy. The primary focus is on romantic love between two people that's emotionally satisfying.

There's nothing wrong with romance. But why focus on fantasy romance when you can experience real romance between you and your husband. When you don't have it, create it. When you want romance and your husband is not meeting that need, tell him and work together to make it happen. When you feel romance is missing, don't go outside of your marriage looking for it because it's not there. Don't allow yourself to be deceived into thinking romance is in any place other than the place God has provided for you within marriage.

Meeting your needs romantically is not solely your husband's responsibility, it's both of your responsibility. You'll have to be honest and transparent and be what each other needs in the marriage (read the song of songs; read about Rebecca and Isaac, Rachel and Jacob, Ruth and Boaz, Esther and King Ahasuerus, and many more). The Bible is replete with romance and love stories.

But before you even approach your husband, go to God in prayer and ask the Holy Spirit to teach you how to romance your husband. Better yet, ask Holy Spirit to help you receive the true romantic love your husband is giving you and you're not seeing it or receiving it. You're missing out on the romance you already have in your own home and in the privacy of your bedroom. The man that married you, your husband, is the one who loves you and is romancing you, but you've been rejecting his romance, unknowingly perhaps, for the fantasy that exists only in your mind. Your husband cannot compete with a figment in your imagination. Ask Holy Spirit to open your eyes to see and enjoy what's in front of you – your loving, romantic, hubby.

Remember, the issues you're having with overwhelming thoughts and desires are all about the brokenness inside of you, not your husband or any other man. After you repent of adultery and covetousness, you will be surprised to know that you have everything you need and want with the man God ordained for you. Ask the Holy Spirit to fix the broken pieces of your life, repair your heart, and fill your void with romance for your husband. He will help you. Here's how I know:

Years ago, I asked Jesus to love my husband through me. I loved my husband, but I wanted him to receive the best love experience possible from me as his wife. How could the love I was sharing with my husband be sufficient for him when my heart was divided, unhealed and broken? My husband is an incredible man, trust me, and I've always enjoyed being his wife. But, honestly, he was getting the short end of the stick for a season in our marriage until after I was delivered from my past. When I repented for holding on to that relationship (in my heart) and renounced it and the sins I committed while in it, I was able to see my husband differently. My eyes were opened, and I liked everything I saw about my husband. God removed the blinders of deceit the Enemy had over my eyes and emotions.

Once, in a dream, which is one method God uses to communicate with me, I saw my husband dancing around in our home. In that dream, I watched him from afar as he danced and danced having a good ole time. I smiled at him as I looked on thinking of how free and happy he seemed and I said aloud, "I like this Terry" (that's my husband's name). He was handsome dancing around so sure of himself and enjoying being with me in our home. I saw a little swag going on with him that I never noticed before. It was like I saw my husband for the first time in that dream. God was showing me that Terry's heart was merry, content, and fulfilled in our marriage. I just needed to join him and enjoy what we had which was so very special.

Between the two of us, neither one of us are skilled at dancing, we've never gone out to party. What I saw in my dream wasn't about the dancing, it was about me realizing that God had already given me the desires of my heart with Terry. I already had the man I wanted who happened to be my husband. God was restoring the romance in our marriage to one that was genuine and pure, which the Enemy had tried to steal with the lie he convinced me to believe. When I woke up from my dream the next morning all I heard in my own voice was, I like this Terry. To this day I still like this Terry.

Don't walk away from a gift God gave you to satisfy the taste of something you think is better. If he's an ex, it's because he wants to be your ex. Remember that, and don't waste your time fantasizing about him. In real life, he won't measure up to your fantasy anyway.

Impure Thoughts. Impure has the same meaning as dirty or something that's not clean. Have you ever heard someone described as having a dirty mind? Impure thoughts are the same thing as a dirty mind.

Let's talk like adults. I want to give you a clear example of impure thoughts. If you cannot experience an orgasm with your husband until you see the face of another man, the ex, or think of a previous sexual encounter with a person, the ex, or anyone other than your husband, I want you to know that's not normal. It's a wrong thought and image, and I don't want you to settle in your mind that it's normal. I don't want you to think nothing can be done to change this because it's not true. God has better for you. God can renew your mind and purify your thoughts.

There is help so don't feel judged because I say it's wrong; I'm just sharing and letting you know so you can be aware and learn how to overcome this attack on your intimacy with your husband. Remember, I had this struggle myself. Because I experienced it I can tell you that it's an ungodly soul-tie with that other person that needs to be broken. There is help for you to become free of this, but most people suffer in silence and have no idea how to stop these images from plaguing their minds.

When you're being intimate with your husband no one should intrude on that moment. If you're having this problem, here's what you do to stop the intrusion. Worship the true and living God before and after each loving moment with your husband. Invite him in and set the atmosphere in your bedroom day and night.

Does this sound over the top to you? It shouldn't. Worldly-minded people invite the Devil into their bedroom all the time through porn, and they welcome all the evil spirits that come along with porn. Why is it strange then to usher in the presence of the Holy Spirit into your bedroom and the purity and holiness that come along with righteousness. Kick the devil out and invite God in.

Realize this, seeing the face of another man, fantasizing about another man, or remembering a previous sexual encounter with another man while you're being intimate with your husband is the same as watching porn. Oh, it's not on the television or cable in your bedroom, but it's flashing across the screen of your mind. Kick that devil out of your bedroom and invite God in. That'll solve that problem. Try it!

Otherwise, your feelings will continue to be manipulated by the memories of the person that you meditate on and also by the images of the person that you allow your mind to continue to see. You can't justify meditating on the memories and focusing on the images of this person any longer. They must go. When you allow this cycle to continue, you're engaging in fantasy and impure thoughts. You must be willing to ask God to purge fantasy and impure thoughts away so you can be sexually healthy. Take the initiative to pay attention to the thoughts that enter your mind and the emotions those thoughts stir up inside of you. Don't just allow them to rule you, get rid of them by casting them down. If you ignore them, they will never go away. Cast them down!

What other option do you have? Do you want to sit around and fantasize about a nonexistent relationship or do you want to move on with your life and be content with the relationship you have that is real and meaningful? Cast those false thoughts and imaginations down!

Do you know how to cast down thoughts and images that keep you bound to ungodly relationships? First, pay attention. What are you thinking or feeling? What are you imagining? Write these things down in your notebook.

Now, prove whether or not what you're thinking or feeling is true or false, right or wrong. If you're thinking or feeling like you belong to a man who's not your husband, then that thought or feeling is false. It's also wrong. Open your mouth and speak the truth. "That man is not my husband and I don't belong to him." Pray it aloud and say that is a lie from the pit of hell and I don't believe it nor will I accept the feeling or thought. It's not true. I cast it down and throw it out of my mind. Speak to God now, and say, Lord, I repent of the very thought and I reject it as a lie from the enemy.

If you sit back and think about times you spent with someone and the fun you had or just the fact you enjoyed being around the person, and that person is no longer in your life by choice, right, then that's the proof you need to no longer sit back and think (fantasize) about them. It's not real according to your proof. Who wants to live their life thinking about stuff that's not real? When you prove those thoughts are wrong you have to take charge and get rid of them. They can no longer be justified and you have the proof to back up the fact that they no longer belong on your mind. If you continue to fantasize, you are believing a lie. Stop doing that.

Refer to scripture and cast down every thought and imagination that does not align with the word of God. Philippians 4:8 says to keep your thoughts continually fixed on all that is authentic and real, honorable and admirable, beautiful and respectful, pure and holy, merciful and kind. And fasten your thoughts on every glorious work of God, praising him always.

Therefore, I encourage you to think about real and kind-hearted people in your life who want to spend time with you and like you as a person and genuinely love you. Embrace them and enjoy them. They are real people that you can see, touch and feel. They are present, not absent. Don't allow yourself to miss out on being with them today, to instead being alone admiring an image or memory that exists only in your head. Enjoy your life! Live, and live fully!

At least now you know and understand that the enemy is working to defeat you with impure thoughts, and the image of that person is being used to trigger you to lust, fantasize, commit adultery, and cheat on your husband. It's a sin trap. Not only that, but the enemy is also stealing your joy and your pleasure. Forgive my slang, but you need to beat his butt with the word of God. Get tough! You got the name of Jesus on your side and if you call on Jesus to help you and rely on his word and power (and obey the word), the enemy will flee from you faster than a jackrabbit being chased by a wolf. This may not be fast enough, but you catch my drift. The enemy will flee!

When you show and prove to the enemy that he cannot have any access to your thoughts, and you fight back with scripture and mean it, he will flee. He will go away and leave you alone.

CHAPTER 8

TRIGGERS

[anything that causes an intense and usually negative emotional reaction in someone]

What's triggering you?

You've been touched by the wrong man, and now you're addicted to his touch. When you engage with a man sexually you form a connection or bond with him. That sexual bond (heavy petting or full intercourse) is not easily broken whether or not it happened within or outside of marriage. It's for this reason God's plan restricts sex for marriage only, between a husband and a wife who love each other and are mutually committed to one another. Nowadays, people don't wait until marriage but it's still the right way and the best way because it's God's way. And, as we know, marriages sometimes end in divorce and when they do the bond between the two remains. That bond is a trigger for you, even after divorce and remarriage or even when you're in a new relationship, it will remain a trigger until you sever the bond. Jumping from relationship to relationship does not sever the bond, it just adds more bonds and more attachments to another wrong man.

In addition to the bond, both flashbacks and residue from the relationship, trigger you emotionally and physically.

Flashbacks

Flashbacks replay in your mind like a scene in a movie. You keep rewinding and replaying the scenes of you and your ex together.

- Do you remember and recall being with him romantically?
- Do you visualize previous sexual encounters with him?
- Do you daydream about anything concerning him?

When you renounce and repent for sexual encounters outside of marriage, God will begin to restore your virtue. Let God heal you emotionally and sexually after a breakup or divorce, and then you will stop visualizing your ex in a way that makes him a movie star in a feature film. You'll be free of flashbacks. Stay in prayer and ask God to renew your mind and remove the soul-tie you have with this person. Be consistent in prayer, don't entertain thoughts of your ex in this way, and the flashbacks will go away. But you can't take this lightly; it will take work to get free and you've got to take care of it in prayer and not allow it to linger.

Residue

The residue is that something about the person that remains with you long after the relationship is over. The residue has a hold on you and it keeps the person relevant and significant to you.

How will you know when the residue is gone?

- Does it matter who the next person is that your ex decides to date or marry?
- Does it matter what your ex thinks of you or say about you?
- Do you feel some type of way (negatively or positively) when you walk into a room and notice your ex is there? Does seeing him bother you (negatively or positively)?
- Deep down, do you wish you could still be close to your ex and hope there's a slight chance you may get back together?

When you reach a point emotionally to where these things don't matter to you and don't hurt you or stir up any emotions at all, then you're free. When you still care about these things go back into prayer and ask God to remove the residue. Stay in God's presence until ALL the residue is gone.

WHAT TO EXPECT WHEN GOD PURGES THE HEART

Pray

Heavenly Father, in Jesus' name, I come to you for help. You said I can cast my cares and concerns on you because you care for me. You said that if I come to you, you will not reject me. You are my help when I'm in trouble. I need you and I put my trust in you to heal my broken heart.

My relationship with this person (say the person's name) has ended. I feel hurt, disappointed and sad about the loss. I still feel love and a connection to this person. Please give me the strength to accept that the relationship is over and help me to release myself from the emotional and physical bond that formed.

I repent for all the sins I committed against you while I was in this relationship. Thank you for your forgiveness, mercy, and grace. Now, I ask you to purify my mind of all flashbacks from my time with this person and remove all the lingering residue of him from my thoughts, emotions, and body. We are no longer a couple. It's over. I pray that you help me to move forward without looking back or reaching back.

Father, reach deep into my soul and close the door to that relationship never to be reopened again. I draw close to you. I invite you to come and fill the empty places in my heart and soul with your Holy Spirit and your love. I need you to help me every day and every hour until my heart is completely healed. Thank you, Jesus, for hearing and answering my prayer. Amen.

Emotions

Remember those private notes you wrote down in your journal? These feelings and thoughts are triggers too:

- Disappointed and anxious
- Hurt
- Abandoned
- Rejected
- Unloved
- Unworthy
- Lonely
- Like a failure
- Not good enough
- Like I want to change his mind
- Life is not worth living
- Like escaping the pain
- Like I did something wrong
- Like, no, it's not over

The feelings are real. Take them into your prayer closet so God can bring healing. But don't entertain these thoughts by dwelling on them when they come. That's what the enemy wants you to do. Daughters of God, you are fighters, you are overcomers.

Hear the Father's voice...

Arise from despair, my daughters. Wake up to the truth of who you are in me and live. For I am here to stir you up and bring you out of depression and hopelessness. I am here to push you forward to the life that awaits you, the good life. Don't sleep, don't allow your soul to sleep, for this is the day that your Lord has made rejoice and be glad in it. Your life is not over, it is only the beginning and I have plans for you. This will not take you out. Look to me. Come to me. Lay your disappointments and hurts upon me and take the joy I give to you. For I am the God who satisfies your soul. I am the God who loves you with an everlasting love. It is not in my nature to reject you or forsake you. Put your trust in me and learn of me. Draw close to me, and I will give you the desires of your heart. I will make you whole and new and you will be refreshed in your spirit. Daughters, you are worthy and valuable that's why I gave my life for you. You are beautiful and the apple of my eye. I made you unique and special, and everything I made is good says the Spirit of the Living God.

Personal Prayer Points

When you go into your prayer closet, read these scriptures aloud. Pray them back to the Father. Lord, you said...

- I should give all my worries and cares to you. (1 Peter 5:7)
- Your unfailing love will comfort me (Psalm 119:76)
- Even if my father and mother (or ex) abandon me, you will hold me close (Psalm 27:10)
- You will never abandon me (Hebrews 13:5)
- You are close to the brokenhearted; you rescue those whose spirits are crushed. (Psalm 147:3)
- The Holy Spirit will help me in my weakness. (Romans 8:26-27)
- Nothing can ever separate me from your love (Romans 8:38-39)
- Put my hope in you (Psalm 42:11)

CHAPTER 9

UNDERSTANDING THE DIFFERENCE LOVE AND LUST

There are multiple relationships in the Bible that give insight into the difference between love and lust. We will focus on three very different examples of what was perceived to be love stories. In two of the relationship examples the men saw who they wanted and had to have the woman, without consideration for anyone else but themselves. They both were undisciplined and self-seeking in their pursuits. On the other hand, for the other relationship, God was asked to be involved, lead, and guide and to make the decision for who the man should marry.

These stories are told for our benefit, I believe, to teach us the outcome of ungodly relationships, actions, and behavior and to show us that lust is the opposite of love. Lust has a negative meaning, and the result of out-of-control romantic feelings of lust brings despair, discontentment, and guilt. On the other hand, love is a positive emotion that is not self-centered. With it (love) comes happiness, contentment, and fulfillment. Let's read the story of Isaac and Rebekah, David and Bathsheba, and then Amnon and Tamar.

Isaac and Rebekah

Genesis 24

The relationship between Isaac and Rebekah is special. I say this because Abraham, Isaac's father, was prayerfully involved in the two of them meeting. He trusted God to choose a wife for his son and sent his servant to find her saying, "God will send his angel ahead of you to get a wife for my son." Next, the servant prayed and asked God to make his search go smoothly. The servant wanted to easily identify the woman God picked for Isaac. He asked God to have the woman say these words … "Let her say, 'drink, and I will give water to your camels also'.

True enough, when he met her and she said these exact words, he knew she was the one. Choosing her for Isaac's wife wouldn't be a mistake. After he prayed to God first, he watched her and was silent as God confirmed that she was the one he chose. God made it plain, indisputable, that Rebekah was his choice. When Rebekah was asked did she want to go to marry Isaac, she agreed willingly after hearing that God specifically selected her for him. When Isaac saw her for the first time he accepted her and married her. The story goes on to say that Isaac loved her.

Isaac's and Rebekah's union brought happiness, contentment, and fulfillment to the entire family and Isaac truly loved her. Why? Because God knew what would make him happy, what he needed, what he wanted, and God knew Rebekah had a pure and kind heart that set her above the rest. You may look for a man who's good looking, tall and slim or with massive muscles, but God is looking at his heart. You may choose someone based on a lustful desire. But God chooses our mates based on the person's character. Not only that, God has a purpose for your life and I want you to realize that the spouse he chooses for you will also fit that purpose.

How many of you would trust God to pick your husband? How many of you would trust God's choice, and submit to his choice, before you ever laid eyes on the man he chose? How many of you want your parents to pray for your spouse or would value this type of involvement in your relationship? That's a rhetorical question but think about the outcome of this marriage and how much it blessed two people who didn't even know each other and probably didn't have marriage on their minds at the time. God chose the mate and the timing for them to marry.

Isaac and Rebekah were never boyfriend and girlfriend. They didn't live together to see how things would work out first. They didn't know if they would satisfy each other sexually first and then tie the knot. They were not engaged for three to five years before marriage. None of that foolishness played part in their union. God did it his way (relationships work best when God establishes them his way). And, guess what, they were very, very happy. Go figure! That should tell us something right there. Amen.

Stop trying to keep your parents out of your 'business' and let them pray to God on your behalf. Let God guide you to the right person while you pray, watch and be still. Finding the right love takes patience while God does the work to join a man and woman together.

David and Bathsheba

2 Samuel 11:2-7 (NCV)

One evening David got up from his bed and walked around on the roof of his palace. While he was on the roof, he saw a woman bathing. She was very beautiful. So David sent his servants to find out who she was. A servant answered, "That woman is Bathsheba daughter of Eliam. She is the wife of Uriah the Hittite." So David sent messengers to bring Bathsheba to him. When she came to him, he had sexual relations with her. (Now Bathsheba had purified herself from her monthly period.) Then she went back to her house. But Bathsheba became pregnant and sent word to David, saying, "I am pregnant."

2 Samuel 11:14-15 (MSG)

In the morning David wrote a letter to Joab and sent it with Uriah. In the letter, he wrote, "Put Uriah in the front lines where the fighting is the fiercest. Then pull back and leave him exposed so that he's sure to be killed."

King David desired Bathsheba even though he knew she was married. He had sex with her, not based on love, but lust. He did not care that she was Uriah's wife, and the story goes on to tell us that David killed Uriah to cover up the fact that he impregnated Uriah's wife. In essence, David's lustful desire once fulfilled brought destruction to Uriah, his murder, and it also led to the sickness and death of the baby between David and Bathsheba. David's behavior brought on a curse to his family that extended way beyond the day of sin. It's not ironic that David's son Amnon behaved similarly to his father, but with his sister. Let's read about Amnon…

Amnon and Tamar

2 Samuel 13 The Message (MSG)

Sometime later, this happened: Absalom, David's son, had a very attractive sister. Her name was Tamar. Amnon, also David's son, was in love with her. Amnon was obsessed with his sister Tamar to the point of making himself sick over her. She was a virgin, so he couldn't see how he could get his hands on her. Amnon had a good friend, Jonadab, the son of David's brother Shimeah. Jonadab was exceptionally streetwise. He said to Amnon, "Why are you moping around like this, day after day—you, the son of the king! Tell me what's eating at you."

"In a word, Tamar," said Amnon. "My brother Absalom's sister. I'm in love with her."

"Here's what you do," said Jonadab. "Go to bed and pretend you're sick. When your father comes to visit you, say, 'Have my sister Tamar come and prepare some supper for me here where I can watch her and she can feed me.'"

So Amnon took to his bed and acted sick. When the king came to visit, Amnon said, "Would you do me a favor? Have my sister Tamar come and make some nourishing dumplings here where I can watch her and be fed by her."

David sent word to Tamar who was home at the time: "Go to the house of your brother Amnon and prepare a meal for him."

WHAT TO EXPECT WHEN GOD PURGES THE HEART

So Tamar went to her brother Amnon's house. She took dough, kneaded it, formed it into dumplings, and cooked them while he watched from his bed. But when she took the cooking pot and served him, he wouldn't eat.

Amnon said, "Clear everyone out of the house," and they all cleared out. Then he said to Tamar, "Bring the food into my bedroom, where we can eat in privacy." She took the nourishing dumplings she had prepared and brought them to her brother Amnon in his bedroom. But when she got ready to feed him, he grabbed her and said, "Come to bed with me, sister!"

"No, brother!" she said, "Don't hurt me! This kind of thing isn't done in Israel! Don't do this terrible thing! Where could I ever show my face? And you—you'll be out on the street in disgrace. Oh, please! Speak to the king—he'll let you marry me."

But he wouldn't listen. Being much stronger than she, he raped her.

No sooner had Amnon raped her than he hated her—an immense hatred. The hatred that he felt for her was greater than the love he'd had for her. "Get up," he said, "and get out!"

"Oh no, brother," she said. "Please! This is an even worse evil than what you just did to me!"

But he wouldn't listen to her. He called for his valet. "Get rid of this woman. Get her out of my sight! And lock the door after her." The valet threw her out and locked the door behind her.

This story is heartbreaking in many ways because so many lives were devastated by their actions. You see clearly how one man's confusion about love destroyed the life and sanity of an innocent woman Tamar. Amnon was attracted to her and obsessed with her, his half-sister. He was so in love with her, he thought, that he was physically sick (lovesick) because he couldn't find a way to be with her intimately.

The enemy sent Jonadab to help him figure out how to do wrong. Jonadab represents the voice of the enemy whose assignment is to whisper in your ear. Jonadab's are scheming, devious, sneaky people you trust like family, close friends, neighbors, and either someone in your circle or someone who knows how to get in your circle. Watch out for people who want to know your secrets. They are Jonadab's. They flatter you, find out what's bothering you, and then show you how to become like them, cunning. He taught Amnon how to be streetwise and cunning like him. Watch out for people who will teach you how to sin. Ask God to help you identify all the Jonadab's in your circle and when he does, stay far away from them. Stay away from Jonadab's! They are not your friends.

As a result, Amnon's view of love caused him to rape his sister. Minutes later, after the rape, he hated her more than he loved her; he hated the very sight of her. Amnon's actions and behavior were not love-based, but lust-based. His actions did not bring him happiness, it brought guilt and discontentment to him and it brought shame and guilt to Tamar and ruined her life. She had no husband nor children and never recovered from the trauma. He ruined her life.

Your feelings will destroy you and others when they are out of control. You don't want lust to destroy your marriage. Single daughters, unmarried, you don't want your lust to hurt people and destroy your relationships. You don't want to ruin your testimony for Jesus over your lack of understanding the difference between love and lust, do you? If you do, the enemy will accuse you unworthy and unfaithful before God, he will ruin your relationship as a Christian so that you will not be believed when you share the good news of Jesus Christ. That means the person that God wants to use you to witness to will not receive you when your reputation is damaged and the news is out about your past. They will not listen to you at all. Is that what you want?

Pray, Heavenly Father, you know what's best for me. Please choose the man I should marry. I ask you and welcome you to choose. Forgive me for trying to find love on my own. I don't want a lustful relationship, I want love, a husband to love me like Isaac loved Rebekah. Give me a loving and kind heart, the right heart, to prepare me for my husband. In Jesus' name, I pray.

WHAT TO EXPECT WHEN GOD PURGES THE HEART?

A TRUSTED FRIEND

CHAPTER 10

NO MORE SECRETS

A secret is something hidden. It is something that is kept from the knowledge of others. We all have secrets, but what's special about having a relationship with Jesus Christ is secrets are no longer necessary. Instead, everything between you and God can be out in the opened, revealed, and settled.

You have secrets that bother you, but you will no longer keep quiet about them thinking you can handle them alone. Secrets can become major problems that nag at you for a long time when you don't deal with them. Here are a few ways we tend to deal with problems instead of getting the available help:

- We hide them
- We deny they exist
- We are ashamed and embarrassed by them
- We are troubled by them
- We are confused by them
- We don't trust anyone to know about them
- We allow them to linger to no end

I get it. Some issues are too private and you don't want others to know about them for that reason. Truth is, if you share your secrets or problems with the wrong people, they gossip, judge, or never let you live it down if you've done something terrible, if something bad has been done to you, or if you're struggling with an issue. So how can you get the help you need if you can't freely discuss your secrets or pinpoint what's wrong?

In 1 Peter 5:7, we are told to cast all of our anxiety upon God because he cares for us. Anxiety is defined as nervousness, worry, concern, unease, or apprehension. So, any secret or problem you have, rely on this scripture and cast it upon God. Anything (meaning ALL the things) you are nervous, worried, concerned, uneasy, or apprehensive about you should cast those things upon God. What does it mean to cast them upon God?

It means to invite God into your heart, mind, soul, emotions (the areas where those secrets or problems exist). How? The same way you invite a friend into your home you invite him into your heart. Let him know he's welcomed. Speak to him and say, Lord Jesus, you said to cast my concerns about *(this thing)* onto you because you care for me. I can't help myself in this area, in any area, and I invite you into my life to handle *(this thing)*.

Jesus is a trusted friend. Empty yourself out before him in prayer and expose all secrets. Have a private place in your home like a closet or bathroom, shut the door and tell Jesus everything. Get to talking. Just that simple, and he will take control and begin the process of purging to get to the truth, show you the truth, behind your secrets and he will heal you wherever you hurt.

- Tell him about it
- Ask him for help
- Lay it at his feet and leave it there
- Trust him with it (all of it)
- Allow him to carry the burden of it, not you
- Watch him work it out for your best interest

God wants to be the one to help you as only he can. You've wasted so much time running to people for help and only think of God when all else fails. Yet, he created you and has the answer to every question and the solution to every problem. You don't have to hide your issues from him. He can be trusted with your innermost secrets without condemnation and rejection and should be the first person you run to for help in all of your troubles.

I want to encourage you to be genuine and authentic with God. When I speak of being genuine I mean you don't have to be fake with him as if everything is going well when in reality you feel like your life is out of control. God knows you better than you know yourself. He wants you to be authentic and true to your personality, spirit, or character. He wants you to approach him with no pretensions. You don't have to make-believe with God. He is a God of truth and transparency, and you can relate to him likewise. There is no secret he cannot handle.

Unfortunately, when I was a teen I didn't tell God how I felt about anything; I kept everything inside. To look at me back then you would think I had it all together. I have always been the kind of person to take things as they come, seemingly. I have been rejected by people I love (and still love to this day). I have been lonely, confused, introverted mostly, and insecure just like many of you. I lost years of intimacy and spiritual growth with the Lord because I didn't talk to him about anything deep about me. I thought it was easier to lay things to rest. But now that foggy way of thinking is gone, and I tell God everything. God is here for you and he will help you no matter the issue.

So, when you come to God with transparency expect him to get involved and rescue you. When you are willing to allow the door to your secret place to be opened, he will unlock the door and reveal everything on the other side of it, uncovering all the hidden things you didn't know were there, and God will purge those things away.

CHAPTER 11

RELY ON THE HOLY SPIRIT

Your first point-of-contact for help in any situation (good or bad) is the Holy Spirit. He is the Spirit of Jesus who lives within every Christian.

The Holy Spirit:

- He is your constant companion and friend
- He is your guide, who is with you every day to lead you in the right direction. He knows the plans of God concerning you
- He is the very presence of God living on the inside of you
- He helps you live the way God wants you to live
- He is your Teacher
- He is your Comforter
- He is your Encourager
- He is your Advocator

Fellowship with him every day. Don't wait until you're in trouble to reach out to him, even though when you are in trouble you can rely on him for help. The Holy Spirit is the One who will change you and purge your heart of everything that's not like Jesus Christ.

Brace yourself for the things you will learn. More than likely you are not as clean and pure as you think but do not let that hinder you from being receptive to the purging process. None of us are clean and pure. We all need Jesus to purge away ungodly things in our heart. It's all about uncovering the unknown. If you are ready to learn the truth behind your problems or issues, remember he is a God of truth. Your role is to be genuine and authentic with him so he can reveal the truth. Trust Him and know that you will be better person at the end of it because you will be more like Him.

When I finally reached out to God for help, the truth began to unfold. What I thought was chaos truly was chaos, partly because of my lack of knowledge, understanding, and disobedience, but it was also God orchestrating events and circumstances working behind the scenes to bring up all the junk I stuffed away deep down in my core. The Holy Spirit took me on a teaching journey first so I could understand what was wrong with me. I learned so much from him. When the Holy Spirit teaches, sometimes he uses people as resources to get his message to you. Oftentimes, you will hear him in your Spirit. Ask the Holy Spirit to make you sensitive to his voice so you won't miss what he's saying. In my case, the teachings were so profound there was no way I would have missed it.

PART II

CHAPTER 12

PURGE
WHAT DOES IT MEAN?

Purge means to get rid of whatever is impure or undesirable. It means to cleanse or purify.

Let's merge the definition above to the title of this book.

What to expect when God gets rid of whatever is impure or undesirable in the heart?

What to expect when God cleanses and purifies the heart?

What does this mean to you, the reader?

It means that before you can have a clean and pure heart, God has to get rid of whatever is inside your heart that is unclean, impure and undesirable.

When God is purging the heart he is getting rid of all unclean, impure and undesirable things in your heart to eliminate them.

Why?

So that you can be cleansed.

So you can be purified.

So that after he purges your heart and removes the impure or undesirable stuff, he can then use you to produce fruit for his Kingdom.

What kind of fruit does God want?

God wants us to do his work in the earth; thus, representing him and bearing fruit and more fruit.

Soulwinning is fruit - sharing the good news of Jesus Christ so others will know him and receive salvation through him.

Living a life that is transformed and represents Jesus Christ is the fruit, so others will see and know that we follow Jesus by our Christian character and actions that bring him glory and honor.

CHAPTER 13

PURGE
WHY IS IT NECESSARY?

Think about this analogy for a moment. What is the first thing you do when you purchase a home or a car that has been lived in or used by someone else? After you take ownership of the property you go in (or get in if it's a car) and begin to clean it up to make it fresh and new to your liking.

As the new owner, you don't want to see or be reminded of the previous owner's stuff. If they left behind raggedy furniture, dirty carpet, scratched up walls, a broken stove or refrigerator, you throw those things out and ultimately replace them with your new stuff. If there's a musty odor of mildew or cigarette smoke lingering, you look behind walls and below the surface to find the source of those smells, and then you clean and purify those areas to create an atmosphere that is sanitized and fresh, adding a fragrance pleasant to you. Similarly, that's why God purges Christians.

Before we are saved, we are uncleaned with sin. That's why the blood of Jesus is important. His blood clean and cover sin. Only His blood can do that.

1 Corinthians 6:20 explains that we have been bought with a price. Now that you've chosen to live your life for Jesus, you are the house he purchased. He has moved in as the new owner so to speak.

The Spirit of God indwells you, the Christian. This means his Spirit, the Holy Spirit, lives on the inside of you, and he is cleaning you up and making you fresh and brand new from the inside out.

If you can relate the purchase of a house or car (and the cleaning thereafter) to the purchase of the human spirit, soul and body (and the cleaning thereafter), then you'll get a sensible and clear understanding of why God purges Christians, right? He wants to get rid of those old, unwanted things in your life and replace them with the new stuff that he as for you. Those old, unwanted desires or habits in your life are considered impure or undesirable now that he's the new owner. *(Side note: Of course we can't compare the financial cost of a home or car to the precious blood Jesus shed as he suffered and died on the cross to pay for the sins of the world; just consider this an intentional, rudimentary example to make a point.)*

As God takes you through the purging process, you will become more like him; and you will be able to produce an abundance of fruit. In other words, you will become valuable to God's Kingdom, useable and effective in bringing lost souls to Christ for salvation.

When the souls of your family and friends are lost because they do not know Jesus as Savior, after you are purged, God will use you more to witness to them and others, bringing them into His Kingdom for eternal life and safety.

CHAPTER 14

GOD PURGES THE HEART FOR THREE REASONS

1. ***To clean it out, purify, sanctify.*** To get rid of and remove unwanted things (contaminations, pollutants) hiding within the heart.

2. ***To Prune it***: To dig up, cut-out, and remove the dead and broken things tucked away in the heart. He clips and trims those things away little-by-little so that His light can come in and rejuvenate and restore the heart back to life.

3. ***To repurpose it***: To change our heart so that it aligns with his purpose and for his glory. It makes us God-centered and Kingdom-minded. It makes us mature and effective Christians and equipped to produce fruit (win souls for Christ). God cares about souls; his #1 priority.

In the book of 1 John, verse 1:9, we learn that if we admit that we have sinned and confess our sins, God is faithful and just and will forgive our sins and *cleanse us from all unrighteousness*. There is one thing I want you to realize from this scripture; sin is unclean and it leaves behind pollutions and contaminations [unrighteousness] that must be cleansed.

Who is John speaking to in this verse? Christians. Who does God purge? Christians: those who have confessed sins and are forgiven.

But John is also telling you that God is faithful and just, meaning you can depend on him to do the right thing concerning sin, which is what led him to die on the cross. We were guilty of our sins, but he took our punishment. When we confess our sins, he forgives them and His blood washes away the pollutions and contaminations the sin left behind. The blood of Jesus cleanses us from all unrighteousness.

Purging. A process that occurs **continuously** throughout the life of a Christian.

You may wonder if the blood of Jesus cleansed you from all unrighteousness, why should you need or expect to be cleansed any further? Wasn't the blood of Jesus enough?

The answer to your question is yes, the blood of Jesus is enough. But, I'd like to review 1 John, verse 1:9 from a different Bible version to gain clarification I believe you will find helpful.

If we [freely] admit that we have sinned and confess our sins, He is faithful and just (true to His own nature and promises) and will forgive our sins [dismiss our lawlessness] and [continuously] cleanse us from all unrighteousness [everything not in conformity to His will in purpose, thought, and action]. 1 John 1:9 (AMPC)

This scripture explains that there is a cleansing that occurs after salvation. When we accept Jesus Christ as our Lord and Savior, he forgives our sins immediately, and the blood of Jesus washes away (cleanses) our **spirit-man** from sin **and** all unrighteousness. But God also focuses on those things that do not conform to His will in purpose, thought, and action. We have things that exist in our **soul** (the mind, the will, the emotions) that are not aligned with the mind, will, and purposes of God. Therefore, during purging God is cleansing our **soul** (mind, will, emotions) from all unrighteousness, all pollutions, and contaminations. This is a process that occurs **continuously** throughout the life of a Christian.

For instance, to cleanse our soul in this sense, God will seek out the impurities and toxins within our soul to remove them. Think of old toxic thoughts and imaginations you have that hide in your soul. The word of God teaches us how to clean our thoughts and cast down and reject those imaginations that don't align with his word, and we are to do this continuously until they are removed completely from our minds.

WHAT TO EXPECT WHEN GOD PURGES THE HEART

Think of past relationships you've had that are unhealthy but you hang on to anyway. God will bring closure and sever those relationships and remove the residue those relationships left behind. If the relationships were not healthy, then your emotions tied to the relationship are not healthy.

God's purpose is to renew your mind by cleaning it out, getting rid of old, unwanted, undesirable stuff that he doesn't want in you anymore now that he is the owner of your **soul** (mind, body, and spirit). He eliminates the impure or undesirables one-by-one. He accomplishes this elimination by purging or through the purging process.

God takes action in the purging process to get rid of everything the old tenant (the enemy) left behind, and then he makes you brand new to his liking so that you represent him and reflect the life that resembles him instead of the old tenant. Who is the old tenant? It's Satan, the Devil. When you belong to Jesus, God will kick him out of your soul and everything he has used to contaminate your mind and body.

To summarize what we've discussed so far when you became a Christian your sins were immediately forgiven and you were immediately cleansed from all unrighteousness because of the redemptive work of Jesus Christ on the cross. Your spirit became brand new (spiritually, you are cleansed by the blood). For emphasis, again, understand that there is a continuous cleansing process of your soul (your mind, your will, and your emotions) that you will experience as you grow and mature as a Christian.

God will purge (clean, refresh, and make new) your mind, your will, and your emotions until there isn't anything toxic or impure remaining that behaves like or identifies with the tenant (the enemy of your soul, the devil) who occupied your soul before you accepted Jesus Christ as your Savior. This type of purging will not happen overnight. Although, if you recall Paul's experience on the road to Damascus in Acts, Chapter 9, it is possible to have such an encounter with God and be instantly transformed. Typically, however, you can expect purging of the soul to continue throughout your life as a believer.

As an example, using the home scenario again, when you purchase a home you perform a deep cleaning in the beginning when you move in, but that's not the only time you clean your house, right? Your house doesn't stay spotless forever. Eventually, it's going to collect dust, bugs will come in that you will have to get rid of, dirt will be found in rooms you don't use often, along with spider webs. Similarly, that's how it is with your soul (mind, will, and emotions), it is not nor will it remain spotless from the time you become a Christian. It takes work and effort to gain a renewed mind, which is why purging is necessary.

Another perspective to consider, during the weekday you keep your house neat and tidy as you work for eight hours, five days a week. Chances are you make up your bed and wash the dishes every day. On Saturdays, you have more time so you may reserve dusting, vacuuming and mopping chores for the weekend. Then, as the seasons change from winter to spring to summer there is an element of cleaning that is more detailed from the norm. Consider cleaning in preparation for the holidays like Thanksgiving and Christmas when you know family and friends are coming to visit. You go even deeper with the cleaning and hire professionals to come in for the hard to reach windows, waxing the floors and even to put a fresh coat of paint on the walls. The point I'm driving is that although purging happens, it's different for each person, more extensive for some and not so deep for others. There are seasons in your life when God will do a deep cleaning within your soul. The purging experience is based on how much pollution or contamination has settled into the mind, will, and emotions of the believer and what's going on in that person's life that has influenced their motives, objectives, thoughts, actions or deeds.

Homes are complex; no two homes are exactly alike. Likewise, no two Christians are alike; no two souls are alike. Some homes have attics and basements, great rooms and dens, multiple bedrooms and bathrooms, multiple kitchens, garages and so forth. As Christians, we have different experiences in life that affect the way we think, the way we act, and what we believe; and some of those experiences are minor while others are major, but God is concerned about all of those experiences great or small, and he addresses each of them in his timing and on his terms. One thing we know for sure and that is God is faithful and just and he will do exactly what he promises to do, forgive us and cleanse us from all unrighteousness.

In fact, and this is good news, God knows everything about you and he will purge all those complex areas in your soul. He knows what's on the different

WHAT TO EXPECT WHEN GOD PURGES THE HEART

levels and engrained deep in your soul, and he knows about every hidden and secret thing in the attic and basement of your soul. God has the key to the rooms we've shut closed and not allowed anyone to come into that space. God will gently enter those doors and deal with whatever is behind them. When God purges, he digs deep and goes to those places to reveal what is lurking beneath the surfaces and hiding in crevasses and, one-by-one, he helps us get to a place where we are free from the influences of those things.

As a Christian expect to be purged. Better yet, don't delay, ask God to purge your heart now and look forward to the process. Allow God to take you beyond your salvation experience and purge your soul where all the hidden stuff that sin left behind will be cleansed away; all of the pollutions and contaminations lying dormant will be uncovered.

CHAPTER 15

PURGING TARGETS THE SOUL

You may find this topic repetitive because I've said it all before, but it's important that I make my writing simple so that even the babies, new Christians, will understand. Your soul consists of three areas: your mind, your will, and your emotions, and each part of your soul needs to be purged.

The Mind (needs to be purged)

Your mind is that part of you that thinks and perceives on its own. Your mind determines what you pay attention to, what you take heed to or obey, whether it relates to obeying a person, or following advice or instructions from someone.

The Will (needs to be purged)

Your will is all about you and what you want for yourself. It takes no consideration for what God wants. It controls your decision-making and your choices. Your will is that part of you that rebels against wise counsel and good advice; you refuse to change your will. When you follow or obey your will, you alone are in control. A self-willed person will not yield to God willingly or easily. They have to be broken by experiencing so much trouble and conflict that they finally give up and surrender to God.

One good example of a self-willed Christian is the story of Jonah. Read the book I wrote, *God wants you to know you ain't right, but the Jonah Spirit won't tell you.* You can find it on Amazon in print and e-book. In the meanwhile, in prayer, submit your will to the power of the Holy Spirit so you won't have a stubborn heart towards God's authority and will.

.

WHAT TO EXPECT WHEN GOD PURGES THE HEART

The Emotions (need to be purged)

Your emotions control your feelings of joy, sorrow, fear, hate, love. Your emotions control how you react to situations and circumstances. Don't trust your unpurged emotions. You will respond inappropriately if you react or make decisions based on how you feel. Your emotions will make you hotheaded and reckless.

Example: I feel like I love him so it's okay to have sex with him. NO. That's how the enemy will deceive you, sweet daughter. When you're not married, that's not right.

Example: He cheated on me so I'm going to cheat on him. NO. That's how the enemy will deceive you, sweet daughter. Don't retaliate. Your job is to pray and ask God to heal you and help your husband return to Christ. Even if you're divorced, continue to pray that God will deliver him and save him. Don't return evil for evil. Your unpurged emotions will have you doing crazy stuff.

> For the grace of God has appeared that offers salvation to all people. It teaches us to say "No" to ungodliness and worldly passions and to live self-controlled, upright and godly lives in this present age Titus 2:11-12 (NIV)

In prayer, submit your emotions to the power of the Holy Spirit so you won't respond to situations in the wrong way.

We learned in the previous paragraphs that God cleanses us from all unrighteous, according to 1 John, verse 1:9. But what is unrighteousness? What are these toxins, pollutions, and contaminations that need to be cleansed?

Unrighteousness is anything that is not righteous, not right according to God's standards; not upright or virtuous. The bible describes unrighteousness as wicked, sinful, and evil. Let's insert the meaning of unrighteousness into the definition of the mind, will, and emotions, to help us connect the dots so to speak.

- **The mind** needs to be cleansed from anything within our reasoning, thoughts, feelings, and perception that is wicked, sinful and evil.
- **The will** needs to be cleansed of any decisions, choices, or desires we have that are wicked, sinful and evil.
- **The emotions** need to be cleansed of any feelings we have that are wicked, sinful and evil.

If God says in the Bible that something is wrong or evil, then that something is unrighteous (wrong and evil) in his sight. Let's take a look at Galatians 5:19-21 in the Living Bible (TLB):

But when you follow your own wrong inclinations, your lives will produce these evil results: impure thoughts, eagerness for lustful pleasure, idolatry, spiritism (that is, encouraging the activity of demons), hatred and fighting, jealousy and anger, constant effort to get the best for yourself, complaints and criticisms, the feeling that everyone else is wrong except those in your little group—and there will be wrong doctrine, envy, murder, drunkenness, wild parties, and all that sort of thing. Let me tell you again, as I have before, that anyone living that sort of life will not inherit the Kingdom of God.

Do you want to be part of the Kingdom of God? Reread the scripture above. What is it saying to you?

The Bible is our resource to the heart of God. It is there we learn of his thoughts, which are higher than our thoughts, and of his ways, which are higher than our ways according to Isaiah 55. You and I may never understand all there is to know about God, but he has provided us with enough insight that points us in the direction of what he wants and expects from us; most importantly, he points us to his son Jesus Christ, the only one who can save us from sin.

It is the shed blood of Jesus that cleanses our spirit-man and covers our sin and makes us righteous in God's eyes. Then, we must digest the word of God, the

WHAT TO EXPECT WHEN GOD PURGES THE HEART

Bible, to renew our minds so that what we think, believe, desire and feel align with what the Bible says, and as we decide to agree with the Bible, our mind is changed and our souls are transformed. Romans 12:2 in the NLT version says don't copy the behavior and customs of this world, but let God transform us into a new person by changing the way we think. Then we will learn to know God's will for us, which is good and pleasing and perfect.

When you believe what God says versus what you think or what the world of popular opinions think, then you agree with God and you are on your way to a renewed mind. When your actions and behavior change because you agree with God and you follow and obey him, that becomes your evidence of a renewed mind.

And it is by this method your mind becomes cleansed of your old, wrong, contaminated belief system. Now your thoughts align with the truth of God's word. When he revealed the false belief that was in your heart, and you read the truth in his word and saw for yourself that you were wrong, then you decided to submit to what he says above anyone else's opinion, even your own opinion. Purging got rid of that old way of thinking. As you read the scriptures, the Holy Spirit will also purge your will and emotions to show you where you are outside of God's plans.

CHAPTER 16

EXPECT A CHANGE IN ATTITUDE AND ACTIONS

We know we were born with a sinful nature. Everyone that you and I have met in this life has sinned; therefore, neither of us is better than the other from God's perspective concerning our sinfulness or righteousness. No sin is worse than the other. Our righteousness is as of dirty rags in God's view, unless we are covered by the blood of Jesus that cleanses us from sin. Billionaires are contaminated with sin; the most educated scholars and geniuses are infected with sin, presidents of countries living in mansions, the homeless living under bridges, drug addicts, and nuns and priests living in sanctuaries are polluted with sin. Romans 3:23 tells us we all have sinned and we all fall short of God's glory.

It doesn't matter if you are the CEO of a Fortune 500 company or working as a cashier at McDonald's, you don't know your own heart and you can't figure it out for yourself what's lurking beneath the surface of your heart. If you haven't asked God to show you what's in your heart, you have no idea. As someone who asked to be purged, I can vouch that when you ask you will be surprised to learn the truth. We can pretend to know or think we know ourselves, but the only true way to discover the truth of who we are is to ask God to reveal it. Only God knows the true heart of a man or a woman.

You see that! God searches the heart and examines the mind. He gets to the root of our nature and reveals our true selves. If you want to know yourself (I mean REALLY want to know yourself) ask him to purge your heart. Mark 7:21-22 teaches that there are 13 attitudes and actions that come out of the human heart. Expect God to reveal several, if not all, of these attitudes and actions hiding in the innermost part of your heart:

1. Evil thoughts
2. Sexual immorality
3. Theft
4. Murder
5. Adultery
6. Greed
7. Malice (mean/cruel)
8. Lewdness (obscene/vulgar)
9. Envy
10. Slander
11. Arrogance
12. Deceit
13. Folly (foolishness)

Most of us are attracted to and intrigued by these things. Why do I say this? Because this is what we engage in privately and publicly. In our private homes, we watch hours upon hours of television shows and movies themed with these attitudes and actions. We listen to music and sing lyrics promoting these attitudes and actions. We place high standards on these things and if a show does not contain them, we don't watch or we classify them as not good or boring. Me too, I've done this as well. I've watched programs over the years where I simply liked the storyline and became a fan of the show. The messier the show the better the program and the more I watched. I'm not here to condemn anyone so don't feel that way. Lately, I've noticed my attitude has changed. When I begin watching a show I find myself fast-forwarding past the sinful stuff or flipping the channels back and forth trying to avoid the part I find appalling. The Holy Spirit within me cannot tolerate it, I just turn it off or move on to something more appropriate. I'm no longer interested in watching and being entertained with sin. It doesn't feed my spirit. My heart has been and is being transformed every day, and I'm at a place in my walk with the Lord that what I watch on TV matters to me because it matters to him.

CHAPTER 17

EXPECT A CHANGE IN MOTIVES AND INTENTIONS

Let's take a look at Simon in Acts 8:9. He was an infamous sorcerer who performed magic, practiced astrology and worked many wonders that impressed people in his community. But his abilities came from the enemy Satan, not God. When Simon heard the disciple Philip preaching the gospel of Jesus Christ he became a believer like many others and was baptized, and then he followed Philip everywhere astonished by the great signs and miracles the Holy Spirit performed through him.

Simon was a believer with a problem because his mind needed to be renewed. The residue of his former life as a sorcerer remained in his heart after he became a believer, and he wasn't fully committed to Christ. We know this to be true because when Simon saw the apostles Peter and John lay hands on believers and the believers received the Holy Spirit, he wanted the same ability and power to lay hands on people so they would receive the Holy Spirit. He offered the apostles money in return for obtaining the power.

Instead, he was rebuked and told his heart was not right, his thoughts were not right, his attitude and his actions were not right. Was Simon a believer in Jesus Christ and accepted the gospel? Yes. But his heart needed to be purged. Simon wasn't aware of the darkness lurking beneath the surface of his heart, but God used his true apostles to reveal it to him. Through purging, Simon not only learned his heart contained wickedness and jealousy but that he was still captive to sin. The desire for vainglory was still a part of his character and lingered in his heart. Simon wanted to maintain the prestige he was accustomed to in his old life as a sorcerer; he was a hustler and wanted to make money as he had done previously, but this time he wanted to use the power of the Holy Spirit to satisfy his ambitions.

The Holy Spirit used the apostles to chastise Simon and reveal the dark motives hiding in him, and they warned him to repent and ask for forgiveness. After Simon was made aware of the condition of his heart, he listened and asked for intercession. Simon's immediate response to the apostles showed a change of heart because he could have walked away and returned to his old life, but he didn't. He could have hated them for the rebuke or he could have become defensive, but he didn't. He humbled himself and asked for prayer.

The apostles didn't reject Simon because of his mistake, they used it as a teachable moment and warned him of what he could lose because of it – the ability to share in ministry. To share in the ministry he needed the Holy Spirit for real, and the only way to receive the Holy Spirit is by genuinely repenting and asking for forgiveness.

Like Simon, we need the Holy Spirit for real. Purging will remove all of your wrong motives and intentions that you may not know exists in your heart and you will be chastised and rebuked. Don't get defensive with God and rebel. Humble yourselves and get ready for this and ask for prayer that you yield to the Holy Spirit instead of yielding to your ambitions and wants.

What to Expect When God Purges the Heart

Being purged is not easy.
It's a hard thing to discover the truth about yourself; ask God for a heart of humility to receive the truth.
You may think you're going crazy, but you're not.
God is exposing the junk within you so he can remove it.
Ask God for a heart of repentance
Jesus walks with us through the purging process.
You're safe in the hands of Jesus but hold on tight.
All believers and followers of Jesus Christ
should want to be purged.
Before you judge me, ask God to purge your heart and see what happens.
Pray in Tongues, allow Holy Spirit to pray through you.
You may lose friends.
You may be misunderstood.
God purges us because he loves us.
We experience his love, compassion, discipline, warnings, long-suffering, patience, and help.
You must go through the purging process
to become a person God can use for His glory.
In the end, after the purge, you come out like pure gold!
You learn how much you need Jesus.
You learn obedience.
You learn to surrender.
It's worth it!

Be prepared for multiple purges in your life; it doesn't just happen once.

WHAT TO EXPECT WHEN GOD PURGES THE HEART

Call upon me in the day of trouble; I will deliver you, and you shall glorify me.
Psalm 50:15 (ESV)

I believed the Lie. For so long the Lie gave me hope and I felt that if I held on to the Lie with all my heart and soul, that one day the Lie would become the Truth. Every day of my life since the age of ten I have thought about the Lie. Immediately, at an instant, without really knowing when or understanding why, the Lie meant everything to me. And although I couldn't always reach out and touch it, nor could I hear its voice, I trusted it and loved it ever so much. I kept the Lie in a place I thought was safe, in my heart and in my soul. And even after the seasons of time, I still yearned for and needed the Lie.

When the Lie was near me I felt complete. Even when there was silence between us I was content. I was pleased just to be in his presence, to watch and admire him. I studied his ways and I listened to his heart until I felt I knew his thoughts. Everything I wanted was in the Lie. He was strong in character, so sure of himself. Over the years he had become my hero. We spent time together and we were happy for a time, at least I thought. When I needed to laugh, the Lie gave me laughter. And when I began to cry, the Lie inspired each tear. I was consumed with passion for the Lie. My heart was sold out completely, no space for anyone else. I was youthfully in love and all was well within.

Trouble! I don't want it! Distance! Come back! He's not telling me, but I know his thoughts. He's here with me but far away. I don't know what to do or what to say. There's a battle going on that I can't fight. I don't know how to handle this trial and I'm so scared. I feel lost because I'm watching his struggle and I'm silent. He knows I'm hooked and he cares, but he's not happy. I'm frustrated and angry because he has changed. He's not telling me he wants to go, and I don't know how to ask him to stay. I won't question him and make him talk even though I know what's wrong. If I ask the question, he will tell me the truth. I dare not ask because I didn't want to hear what I already knew. I said nothing and allowed him to continue in struggle.

One day I realized that the Lie wasn't holding on to me any longer. He had left. He had moved on so very long ago. I had been wrestling with the Lie in my soul. Somehow the Lie conquered my heart and took residence in my soul. He had touched a place so deep inside of me that I could not reach. He had let go of me, but I held on to him for dear life.

I called for the Lie to come back to me. I asked without saying a word. He called just to say hello and to keep in touch. Visits were few but surprising and pleased me greatly. I was driven to get the attention I so desperately needed from the Lie. With a pounding heart and satisfied soul, I interpreted the visits as hope. Hope encouraged me and gave me patience. With hope and patience standing on either side of me holding my shaken hands, I waited and waited. I hoped and waited until I dozed off into a deep, deep sleep.

Twenty years later I awoke to warfare, spiritually unprepared for battle. I tried to separate myself from the Lie. "Go away!" I said. "I want Reality." Time and time, over and over, again and again, I said, "Go away, I want Reality." When I wouldn't listen to the Lie during the day, I would dream dreams of the Lie during the night.

PART III

CHAPTER 18

PURGE MY HEART I'M A WOMAN IN CRISIS

It was nearly a year after our beloved Pastor E. L. Thomas Sr. passed away when my husband and I decided to move our church membership to one of our fellowship churches located nearby. We worshipped with this church and visited many times with our pastor and church family so it felt like home when we joined. I was an interpreter for the Deaf at my home church before our move.

Approaching a year into our membership, the pastor asked if I would lead a Deaf ministry. He knew I was an interpreter because I ministered at his church before I became a member. I came with a guest interpreter who was a friend of mine; I was there to assist her. As a new member of his congregation, it made sense that God would have me continue to serve in this capacity so I agreed.

One Sunday morning after about the third year of ministry, I was standing on the pulpit interpreting the sermon. My new pastor, also beloved, preached a message I found intriguing because it clicked with something within me that needed to hear what he was saying. In that instant, I was learning, and there was a shift in my level of understanding as he continued delivering the message. I knew God was speaking to me at that very moment.

WHAT TO EXPECT WHEN GOD PURGES THE HEART

The Holy Spirit uses Pastors, Teachers, and Ministers of the Gospel

The pastor talked about soul-ties, and he spoke to people like me who had been troubled by a secret for a long time. He talked about having thoughts, emotions, and issues that we have but cannot share with others – at least not in a completely honest way. Some things you can't talk to anybody else about but God, he said. He discussed the need to be delivered from that one thing you can't seem to get rid of in your life [he emphasized *that one thing*]. In the sermon, he used words like "oppression, bondage, and deliverance," and the need to be set free in your mind.

I knew I was troubled about a relationship from my past, but I didn't know how to articulate the extent of that trouble nor did I know who I could trust with the knowledge of how it was affecting me, even though many years had passed. At the time, I didn't understand why the experience persisted in my mind, and for the life of me, I didn't know how to resolve it or move passed it.

Before this sermon, I had no idea I was oppressed by the enemy of my soul, the devil, who was aggressively overwhelming my emotions and keeping me in bondage to my past. The word bondage means to be in a place of servitude or *to be a captive*. The thing I secretly struggled with, that one thing, had power over me emotionally and I became a slave to that one thing (in my mind). The pastor's terminology that day gave meaning and understanding of the frustration I faced regularly and had struggled with for many years. This was a serious matter because I was still longing for the person I lost due to a breakup when I was a teenager; that longing was nagging at me all the time - it was a deep-rooted and distressing problem.

This sermon addressed my deep-rooted problem as I stood on stage interpreting. The Holy Spirit spoke to a desperate place within me and I was finally getting revelation and breakthrough understanding that described both my inner conflicts and the darkness working behind the scenes creating them. The Holy Spirit helped me to see clearly that I had a soul-tie lingering from my past, and that the soul-tie was ungodly. The enemy used the unresolved issues concerning the breakup to keep the emotions from my past alive. How was he doing that? He targeted my mind through thoughts and images. The enemy was working behind the scenes, in the background of my memory, and he was replaying all the real events, conversations, and encounters I had with this person. Only he was making the events, conversations and encounters bigger and more meaningful than what they were. I was being oppressed by my worst enemy.

> ***The LORD also will be a refuge for the oppressed, a***
> ***refuge in times of trouble.***
> ***Psalm 9:9 (NKJV)***

First, I want you to know that I am a Christian, a believer and follower of Jesus Christ. The first time I accepted Jesus Christ, I was about 8 years old. I chose to live my life for Jesus again, for the second time, as a teenager.

I was a regular churchgoer who occasionally hosted in-home Bible studies. I attended Bible study at church, Sunday School classes during my teenage, young adult, and adult years. I co-taught classes alongside my husband, an ordained minister of the gospel.

Growing as a Christian, reading the Bible and praying was my lifestyle, and a relationship with Jesus is my heart's desire to this day. I loved Jesus, and I was faithful in ministry. But none of those activities stopped the enemy from bothering me. Instead, I was his prime target long before my salvation experience. He had an ace in the hole from my childhood that had not been renounced, which is why I was having problems as an adult. Hear my point as I reiterate that reading the Bible, praying, loving Jesus and being faithful in ministry did not stop the enemy from targeting me and it will not prevent him from targeting you. He will never win against you, but he will bother you.

He, the enemy, was using his legal right to influence an area in my thinking and oppress me both emotionally and physically because of that soul-tie. He was able to keep me stuck and unable to move forward to enjoy life as God intended because I was unaware of his tactics (in this area) and I didn't have the know-how to stop him in his tracks. However, in this sermon, the Holy Spirit was actively educating me like a child in grade school, teaching me basic vocabulary and definition on the spot and giving me the words I needed to speak during my private prayer with him. The Holy Spirit let me know I was being oppressed.

But what does that mean, being oppressed? In my case, it's exactly what I described above as a deep-rooted issue. It meant I was constantly being reminded of a person who once held a special place in my heart but was no longer in my life. There was a relentless replay of fond memories lurking in my thoughts practically every day. The relationship was dead. But the emotions and memories tied to that relationship were still alive and real.

One would think that eventually, I would shake off my past and those memories, but they both had become a natural part of who I was as a person. Unfortunately, a specific way of thinking had been formed in my mind and nurtured from when I was very young and innocent; and this form of thinking had become habitual and controlling in nature. I needed to be delivered from the oppression.

> *The Spirit of the Lord GOD is upon me, because the LORD*
> *has anointed me*
> *to bring good news to the poor; he has sent me to bind up*
> *the brokenhearted,*
> *to proclaim liberty to the captives, and the opening of the*
> *prison to those who are bound*
> *Isaiah 61:1 (ESV)*

To uncover and undo areas in my life where the enemy was hiding and working his evil deeds behind the scenes, I needed deliverance.

Deliverance means I needed to be rescued, I needed to get relief, I needed to escape captivity and I needed to be freed from bondage linked to this past relationship.

Applying this definition to my situation, the Holy Spirit began to reveal the answer to these questions to initiate the deliverance process:

1. How did the enemy gain the legal right to influence my thinking?
2. How do I expel him from my thoughts, and take that legal right from him?
3. How do I break free from the soul-tie?
4. How do I ensure the enemy never bothers me about this again?

When the Holy Spirit gave me the answers to these questions, **and I accepted his answers as truth**, then he was able to start the process of purging away the toxins, pollutions, and contaminations in my mind. He cleansed, refreshed, and made my mind brand new based on truth – giving birth to what was real and burying what was a lie.

So the enemy oppresses us based on lies we believe, but it is God who delivers us from those oppressive lies and beliefs through purging, and that leads to freedom from oppression. It is the Holy Spirit who helps us through this process by revealing truth and helping us understand what's going on.

In retrospect, the enemy didn't own me and never will. I belong to Jesus Christ. However, I was the enemy's captive and I was imprisoned by the secrets of my heart. The Holy Spirit knew I was desperate and he understood, and even though I could not articulate my issue, he knew exactly what was wrong and what I needed. The Holy Spirit chose the time and the place, and he initiated the sermon as the start of his rescue plan for me.

The Holy Spirit uses co-workers, friends, and people you can relate to

I believe the Holy Spirit wanted to help me months earlier when a co-worker invited me to her church. She told me they were having a deliverance service and thought that since I was a Christian I may want to come to the service. Christians are saved from sin and destruction but we can have demons harassing us, she explained. She shared with me ways demons came out of people. She said that some people fall out onto the floor and start foaming out of the mouth, some get runny noses or begin to sneeze, or some may start squirming around on the floor. This all sounded scary to me quite frankly. I figured if I had a demon, I didn't want to be clowning around in church and throwing up foam.

WHAT TO EXPECT WHEN GOD PURGES THE HEART

I didn't want to act like that, and I was kind of afraid to find out if I had a demon. That's a scary thought if you've ever seen the movie, The Exorcist, which is all I could think about when she started talking about demons.

I remember thinking that if I were going to have this kind of experience I would prefer to be around family and friends for support. Then, after imagining myself carrying on as she described, I began thinking, if I have demons to make me act like she was describing I would much prefer to be around strangers versus people I know and who know me. I don't want my close friends and family witnessing my head spinning, and then remembering it myself every time I run into them in public *(I'm laughing)*. Lord, forgive my pride! I did not take her up on her invitation, but I now believe I missed an opportunity for the Holy Spirit to teach me about oppression, bondage, and deliverance sooner.

When my co-worker finished talking, I was left with pondering questions ... can Christians have demons living inside of us? How could a demon dwell inside of a Christian where the Holy Spirit dwells? I didn't ask her any of my questions, of course, I just listened intently to her conversation. I was interested but puzzled and lacked understanding at that time.

Growing up, I don't recall hearing or learning about a deliverance service. I was raised in a Baptist church with a strong emphasis on Christian education. Perhaps we called it something else and I didn't fully understand it or participated, but I never saw one person cough up foam or throw up anything in a church service, prayer service or Bible study; that, I know for sure.

Reconsidering, if I knew then what I know now, I would have been at that deliverance service sitting on the front row with my hands raised to God asking, begging and pleading for Him to deliver me and set me free. I would not have cared one way or the other about demon spirits, demonic oppression, throwing up or whatever – I would have trusted in the powerful name of Jesus Christ to come to my rescue through the anointed, Holy Spirit-filled saints there to support me and walk me through the deliverance process. We should never allow fear, shame, nor pride to keep us from the freedom God has available to help overpower the enemy's attacks and the fiery darts he throws at us.

For these reasons, the conversation with my co-worker and the sermon my pastor preached, I studied to learn more about deliverance. Not to go in-depth in this book but understand that demons cannot possess the body of a Christian as they did to the character Linda Blair portrayed in The Exorcist. However, they can oppress and harass our minds through wrong thought patterns and wrong belief systems as I was experiencing, and they can attack our physical bodies through sickness and disease. Demons have no power or authority over us unless we give them power. We give them power through open doors of sin, wrong thinking and desires, wrong ideas, wrong beliefs, and an unwillingness to repent and surrender to the will of God.

The Holy Spirit taught me that when we sin and refuse to repent or don't realize we need to repent, we give demons power and access into our lives. He taught me that when we lack understanding and don't know what sin is according to scripture, and willingly participate in sin out of ignorance, we give demons a welcome mat to walk into our lives and toy with our mind and body. Every time we disobey God in any way we give the devil power to operate in our lives. Every time we believe a lie (whether we realize it's a lie or not) we give power to the enemy, the devil, and as soon as he can use that lie to his advantage and attempt to destroy us and the people we know, he will. So every door of sin, every door of wrong thinking and desires, every door of wrong ideas, and every door of wrong beliefs that we have and hang on to must be closed. Afterward, the enemy loses his access to harass and operate in our lives.

Meanwhile, as we go back to the beginning of my purging experience through the sermon, as the Holy Spirit taught me about oppression, bondage, and deliverance, it was enlightening. On the other hand, it was also devastating. Not only was I bound by demonic strongholds and influences in my life and was being oppressed daily, but I had also been bound for twenty years and I didn't have a clue.

When God began to deal with this bothersome issue in my life I was in my mid-thirties. First, God used the co-worker to introduce me to the term deliverance. Then, he used my pastor to preach a sermon in such a way that I knew, without a shadow of a doubt, that it was me who needed deliverance. Since I could identify with this sermon, I wanted deliverance and was distressed enough in my private life to get it by any means necessary.

Nearing the end of the sermon the pastor said sometimes you need to get crazy before God. Cry out with all your heart and mind and soul, he said, and ask him to move that thing that is bothering you and keeping you all bound up. As a matter of fact, he said, some of you should just take off running for your deliverance. I took this literally.

There I was standing on the pulpit interpreting, but also needing this deliverance. Was I willing to run to get it? If that was all it took to get delivered, then I had to do it. And I did.

I had an odd expression on my face apparently because one of the other interpreters came up and touched me on the shoulders to switch places with me. Perhaps I had stopped interpreting altogether without noticing and stood there in a gaze to listen to the preacher. It's possible. Whatever the case, a switch occurred. Normally, we would never switch during the middle of a sermon, but I know the Holy Spirit sent her to release me.

With that tap on my shoulder, I jumped off the pulpit onto the floor of the church and I ran in desperation (I do not remember gracefully walking down the stairs but, hopefully, that's what I did). I didn't bother to take my high heel shoes off or care about who was watching me; I just ran. All I know is that while I was running full speed I was also praying aloud.

This was the first time I remember crying out to God for help, privately or publicly. I had **asked** for help privately, of course, but I had never **cried out** for help. *(There is a big difference between asking for help and crying out for help.)* The Holy Spirit had just taught me what was wrong with me, and he taught me the language I needed to use to express what was bothering me; so this was my opportunity to ask for what I needed. As I ran around this not so small church I spoke out loud, and as loud as I could, a specific name to ensure all of Heaven heard me. I transitioned from this quiet-spoken, reserved person to someone on a mission. This need was between me and God.

I became the person the Holy Spirit needed me to be all along, genuine and authentic. I unashamedly prayed about what was distressing me. I announced to God that it was a struggle and I cried out for help. "Deliver me from this thing God, remove this burden," I prayed. I mentioned the name of this person in the presence of God, and countless times I repeated help me, Jesus, deliver me, Jesus. Finally, as I arrived back at my seat near the other interpreters I began to give God thanks and praise. I was so serious, so sincere, so needy; and so very desperate. I remember that day well.

Instantly, I received a sense of peace and I felt free like a heavy weight had lifted from my shoulders. All these years I needed relief and never knew who could help me or if help was a possibility. But, I learned there was much more involved in total deliverance than I could have imagined.

WHAT TO EXPECT WHEN GOD PURGES THE HEART

He will make the Levites clean.
He will make them pure, like silver is made pure with fire!
He will make them pure like gold and silver.
Then they will bring gifts to the LORD, and they will do
things the right way.
Malachi 3:3 (ERV)

Deliverance is a process

The following Sunday I ran into my Pastor in the hallway at church. Sabrina, did you get your deliverance, he asked me. "Yes! Thank God I got my deliverance!" I said with assurance and I believed it with all my heart. The entire week from one Sunday to the next was nothing but peace for me. I felt no oppression at all; I was happy and relieved.

Was I delivered? Yes, in the spirit realm God answered my prayer immediately. It was done. In the natural, however, I had to go through a process of purging that was extensive. It involved purging, yes, but it also involved emotional healing from a few other losses I experienced in early childhood. The Holy Spirit took me back to the crib and dealt with all those things I had buried deep within. I had to learn to walk out that deliverance which was a huge challenge within itself.

You see, I had layers and layers of beliefs and wrong patterns of thinking that needed to be purged. I had many open doors of sin that needed to be closed. I had hurts that needed to be healed. I needed to see myself as God saw me at that time, and I needed to learn the role I played in creating the issues that plagued me. I was stubborn about my past and about that relationship. All of this 'stuff' had to be dealt with one-by-one. I had to be dealt with as a child of God in error in many ways that escalated my troubles. On top of myself being a problem, the enemy was not going to let go of me that quickly and that easily. He slowly began to pick a fight.

Little did I know that deliverance for me would be a long process of understanding why I was bound in the first place, discovering why I thought what I thought, understanding why I felt what I felt, learning why I believed what I believed, and discovering why I was longing for something dead. All of those emotions brought unrest into my life and was not in alignment with the will of God.

Spending time with God in prayer and trusting him with all areas of need in my life was needed to become spiritually whole, but I was silently trying to figure out my issues solo. And, when I did talk about it I cast my cares and concerns upon people who couldn't relate to me or understand my plight. We are defeated in specific areas in our life because we don't know how to apply the resource of the Bible, the word of God, to those areas and get the help that we need. I think about the popular phrase I hear people say all the time: the battle is not mine, it's the Lord's; you know the infamous song by Yolanda Adams. But in my case, the battle had been mine and I was losing the battle.

After the sermon, weeks and months passed, and I had no issues. I felt normal. Then, before I knew it the pressure hit, and I discovered the struggle had found its way back. I don't know when or how but those old ways of thinking were back. I felt stuck, depressed and unhappy. I did not know how to rid myself of these all-consuming thoughts that returned with a vengeance.

After my desperate run, after my prayers to the Lord, after months had passed, I was now even more aware of my thoughts. They were stronger and offered no peace. I felt hopeless and defeated. But as time went on I realized something; those feelings of hopelessness and defeat were emotions from the enemy, they were not from God.

WHAT TO EXPECT WHEN GOD PURGES THE HEART

Wash me thoroughly from my iniquity,
And cleanse me from my sin.
Psalm 51:2 (NKJV)

The Enemy comes to taunt

One day I was visiting a relative's house. As I was leaving, backing out of the driveway, a neighbor flagged me to stop. I knew him, a friendly neighbor, so I stopped to chat. I cannot remember everything he said, but I do remember mildly fresh statements. He was teasing me, so I was not offended. I told this fresh guy that I was married (which he knew) and that I was a woman who loved the Lord for real and living a life for Christ. His response stunned me. It may not be me, he said, but there is somebody out there you would say yes to. It's somebody, he repeated.

At that moment I realized that person was not the nice and polite neighbor, but an evil spirit speaking through him, and that evil spirit not only knew my struggle, he also knew I was seeking help in this area. The devil got in my face and challenged me that day. As I drove away I realized for the first time that I had encountered a demon and I knew exactly who that demon was referring to; the devil was taunting me. Instead of fighting back and telling the devil he was not going to win and rebuking him, I relented to the feelings I thought were true. Would I? Would I say yes to the person he was referring to? Possibly. With my state of mind during that time, probably.

Here's how I relented. One evening I was at home alone resting on my living room sofa. I began to pray. In a whisper, I said, "God, can I see him?"

I had this bright idea that perhaps a conversation with this person would help to resolve this thing within me and put it to rest. The house was quiet as I listened to hear what God would say but there was no reply. I asked again. "God, can I see him?" Still, there was only silence. Frustrated I asked, "God, do I love him?" In a soft, clear voice I heard God say, "No."

I was bewildered and shook off what I heard God say as if God himself had missed the mark and didn't understand my question. I can remember physically shaking my head as if to stay that cannot possibly be true. I continued this now interesting dialogue with God with a question, "I don't love him? God, what do you mean I don't love him?" There I was doubting God as if He was the one confused. What I felt was love and I knew it, what else could it be?

I believed I loved this person all my life. What other reason would cause my struggle? Why would this situation persist if 'love' was not the root cause of my feelings? Surely I had to be in love with this guy to think of him all the time, I believed.

Bluntly, but in a soft and clear voice, God said, "It's lust."

Lust. Lust. That word echoed around in my head. Did he just say lust? I was shaking my head in total disbelief at what I heard. This was God talking to me right, Sabrina, the virgin on the day she walked down the aisle to marry her husband.

I'm thinking what in the world! Obviously, God was a little off with this one. I loved this person for real. This thing was not about sex or lust, in my mind, it was about the person, the object of my affection, this great guy! How could God use this word to describe me?

I'm a Christian. I knew not to have sex outside of marriage so I didn't. How could I have lust? What is lust?

I didn't take the time to research this at the time, but later, after God healed me, I searched the bible commentary for the answer to what lust is and it's explained this way:

Craving or lusting is more than inappropriate sexual desire. **It can be an unnatural or greedy desire for anything.** *In Numbers 11:34, God punished the Israelites for craving good food. Their desire was not wrong; the sin was in allowing that desire to turn into greed. They felt it was their right to have fine food, and they could think of nothing else.* **When you become preoccupied with something until it affects your perspective on everything else, you have moved from a desire to lust.**

WHAT TO EXPECT WHEN GOD PURGES THE HEART

This thing had grasp so much of me that the desire had become lust. But, there I was thinking God was wrong because I was a virgin on my wedding day; and thus, I couldn't possibly have an issue with lust. But I also knew God cannot lie and He's never wrong.

The truth is I was extremely preoccupied with this person and it did affect my perspective on everything else, especially dating or allowing myself to fully love another person in that way. I thought of or wanted no one else. I loved my husband, but it wasn't 100%. I loved God, but it wasn't 100%. I loved this guy or craved this guy, 100%. I never did let him go from my heart.

On the other hand, sexually, I knew not to go too far and sin, but it didn't mean I didn't want to when we were dating. I knew better so I held back and didn't fully express my desire for him at the time. I contained my emotions sexually. I wanted to wait until marriage and had privately, in prayer, committed myself to God. But the sexual desire was birth back then as teens, not going all the way, but doing just enough to create the desire.

It was that same desire that crossed my mind on my wedding day as I consummated my marriage with my husband. It was dormant until that night. (I speak on my husband in a later chapter, but I want to insert here that my husband knew while we were dating that I still had feelings for my ex and that I had not been fully healed from the breakup. We talked about it before and after our engagement. I contemplated breaking the engagement, but he didn't want that. He knew the issue was all mine and had nothing to do with the other person. His view on the matter was that the two of us could get through this issue together; he thought he could help me move forward.) My problem was bigger than both of us, until we learned to take it to God in prayer.

However, it wasn't too big for God to handle. I invited God into my secret place when I cried out to him for help. But, unconsciously, I was standing in the way of getting the help I sought because I didn't want to face it. So what did God do? The Holy Spirit, the Spirit of Truth, revealed to me what was lurking beneath the surface of my heart. In other words, since I was beating around the bush and praying religious prayers, he decided to speak into my ear clearly so that I could hear him say what was hiding in wait to destroy me if I didn't allow him to purge it.

Daughter, you have a lust problem. The desire for my ex had escalated way beyond the love I once had for him and was now out of control lust and greed. I was blind to the truth of who I was from God's perspective. In Jeremiah 17:9, we learn that the heart is deceitful above all things, and desperately wicked: who can know it? None of us know what's in our heart; it takes the Spirit of Truth, the Holy Spirit, to tell us.

Sadly, the enemy wins until we learn to fight spiritually, and the fight begins when we run to Jesus for help. As a child of God seeking God for help out of despair as I did, expect to be confronted with the truth because God is about the business of delivering you from the enemy's grip so you can be free to do what he has called you to do for his Kingdom.

There I was a grown, married woman with children still dealing with teenage issues, and God saw fit to resolve this problem and had been waiting on me to proactively invite him into my situation.

You may have a secret struggle or an aggravation and have no idea why it exists. It may not be the same as mine, but whatever the root of your issue please know that God will disclose it to you if you ask him. It doesn't matter what you think about yourself (good or bad) or what I thought about myself (good or bad) because we don't know ourselves the way God knows us. All we know is something is wrong and we can't seem to determine the cause. We need to remember that sin resides within our hearts (everybody's) and that's why we need God to transform our hearts. Our ways are not hidden from God; our sin is not concealed from his eyes, according to Jeremiah 16:17. What's important to understand is that many of our problems or issues are related to sin even if they go back as far as our childhood. This statement may be a hard pill to swallow, but I feel strongly that it's a true statement because we were born in sin.

The Holy Spirit lives on the inside of Christians making us brand new from the inside out through purging. I'm sharing my story of how God started the purging process with me. But the purpose of my testimony is to encourage you to cry out to God for yourself to get help in your troubles so he can purge your heart, and when he is finished you will come out as pure as gold.

Purging uncovers sin hidden in the heart

When the Holy Spirit begins purging and uncovers our sin, it's not something we should be ashamed of, afraid of or run from. Purging is a good thing. Look at how God gently uncovered my hidden sin. It was a private moment between Father and daughter (just the two of us). He did not have a prophet call me out before the church congregation to reveal what was lurking in my heart and shame me publicly. He responded to me as a loving parent.

Even when God does use a prophet to confront Christians, he does it lovingly. Consider what happened to King David in 2 Samuel 12:1-7. God sent Nathan the Prophet to have a one-on-one conversation with David.

King David, although a man who loved and worshipped God sincerely, had at one point acted in disobedience against God. He committed adultery and murder. Not only did King David have sin in his heart, but he also used his authority as King to have sex with another man's wife and she became pregnant with his child. To hide his sins, King David had her husband killed. And that's why God sent the prophet Nathan to confront King David to basically say – I know what you did last night!

Read all of 1 and 2 Samuel to learn of David and how God called him a man *after his own heart*. David sincerely desired to please God. He wanted to know God's heart, and he sought after the heart of God just as I was seeking after God with my whole heart. Still, with David and myself and many other Christians, darkness lurked beneath the surface of our hearts. I can assure you from one Christian to another, God will purge your sin and the sooner he does the better off you will become.

Likewise, in my case, God gently revealed the true condition of my heart to me and no one else, as I was sitting there with my eyes bucked wide in shock and denial.

WHAT TO EXPECT WHEN GOD PURGES THE HEART

But don't just listen to God's word.
You must do what it says. Otherwise, you are only
fooling yourselves.
James 1:22 (NLT)

When God reveals something about our character that we don't believe we tend to block that important information. For some reason, we don't expect to hear anything about ourselves that's not good, especially when we THINK we are good people. That's exactly what I did – I blocked the revelation of lust hiding in my heart and didn't deal with it (at that time). And that's exactly what happened to Peter, one of the 12 disciples. In Mark 14:43-72 Jesus told Peter that on that day he would deny knowing him as the Christ three times, while in Peter's mind he would never do such a thing. Peter told Jesus that he would never disown him even if he faced death. Sure enough, in the heat of conflict, Peter disowned Jesus three times, cursing and swearing to make his denial believable.

If I were having a conversation with my mom or a friend and either of them told me I had a lust problem, the first thing I would ask them is why are they saying that about me, and to explain to me in what way have I demonstrated lust. At the very least I would have shown an interest in what was said, acknowledge that I heard what they said, and asked for clarity. Likewise, God provides a safe place for us to be genuine and authentic with him, so when we pray and he answers by telling us the truth, we can dig deeper by asking him for an understanding. In other words, I could have asked the Lord to help me understand why he said I had lust or what have I done that identifies the lust.

The truth is meant to help us not to hurt us. Peter could have said Lord, I don't want to be the type of person to deny that I know you. I could have said Lord, I don't want a lustful heart. Instead, we both responded with denial. The appropriate response should be as easy as letting the Lord know you don't want to be that way, and then asking him for a change of heart. Peter and I could have asked to be purified on the spot.

Instead, when I heard the truth about myself I glossed over it. Why? Because I did not believe what I was feeling was lust; I believed it was love regardless of what God said. This type of thought process is called exchanging the truth for a lie. The reason many of us are still not delivered from strongholds and oppression is that we hang on to lies we believe. I completely ignored the truth, skipped right over it and jumped to my next question for God.

I prayed, "Can I see him?" This soft but firm voice said to me, "Don't touch him."

Don't touch. I repeated. Okay, I won't touch. Then I thought to myself, I can see him without touching him. I took God's instructions as his approval to see him as long as I didn't touch him, and I didn't ask God another thing. This is a prime example of how we miss God. I was in prayer and received instructions. Then, I thought to myself … big mistake! Listen, Eve thought to herself in that garden after the enemy put the wrong thoughts in her head. Our responsibility is to hear God and obey, not think it through until his answer fits what we desire in the first place. When we start thinking things through in our minds, we get it twisted. We are to be doers of the word of God, not hearers only.

How many times have we read the Bible and received instructions from God concerning things he asks us to do and those things he tells us not to do? We read it, hear and understand it, but then do not allow God's word to penetrate us deeply enough to produce a converted heart that leads to obedience. We allow God's word to fall to the ground instead of turning to him with a listening ear and a heart of purpose to follow his instructions. He told me two things: one described a sin issue and the other was a simple instruction to obey. Why didn't I say to God, please deliver me while I had his full attention? That's what I said when I was running desperately around the church that Sunday.

Not following God's instructions is sin

Purging uncovers sin hidden in the heart. God has given us examples in the Bible to teach us *what to do* and *what not to do* when we hear his voice. For example, let's reflect on Adam and Eve in the Garden of Eden in Genesis 2. We know that after God formed Adam from the dust of the ground and breathed into his nostrils the breath of life he became a living soul. God then provided a home for Adam, in a garden that God himself planted. Out of the ground the Lord God made every tree grow that was pleasant to the sight and good for food. The tree of life was there, and then there was another tree – the tree of the knowledge of both good and evil. This is the infamous tree we have all heard about. God told Adam he could eat from any tree in the garden **except for this tree**, the one with knowledge of both good and evil. Hear this, God said in the day that you eat of it you shall surely die. That's very clear, straight to the point warning, and it should have been sufficient enough for Adam to take heed and follow God's instructions.

Now when Eve was made from Adam's flesh and became woman, the two became one. They dwelled in the garden together. Here comes the enemy, on assignment, to entice Eve to **question the word of God and cast doubt on what God means when He gives an instruction**.

> *Genesis 3:1 (AMP) Now the serpent was more crafty (subtle, skilled in deceit) than any living creature of the field which the Lord God had made. And the serpent (The enemy) said to the woman, "Can it really be that God has said, 'You shall not eat from any tree of the garden'?"*

We know the story. Eve began to question the word of God in her heart at the prompting of the enemy.

But I want to point out something very important, and that is Eve knew exactly what God said and she understood exactly what He meant. We know this because of how Eve responded to the enemy. Genesis 3:2 (AMP) And the woman said to the serpent, "We may eat fruit from the trees of the garden, except the fruit from the tree which is in the middle of the garden. God said, 'You shall not eat from it nor touch it, otherwise you will die.'"

Just like Eve, we know the right thing to do especially when God has spoken. We have biblical instructions on what to do and what not to do. But the serpent said to the woman, "You certainly will not die! Genesis 3:4 (AMP). It was then Eve began to look at things differently, in a way that aligned with what Satan said about it versus what God said about it. Eve saw that the fruit on the tree of both good and evil looked good to eat and was pleasing to the eye, and by eating eat she would gain something she thought she lacked or was missing which was wisdom.

And, just like Eve, when a thought pops in your head that differs and opposes what God has said to you, then you know it is the enemy who is at work in your thought-life. He will entice you to question what God meant when he spoke to you and he will make you believe you are missing out on something good. And, it is at this point you have a choice to make and that is to either obey God or disobey God. This is that crucial moment when what is in your heart is revealed. Is your heart surrendered to God? Or is there something in your heart that you want, and probably have always wanted, and now is your opportunity to go after it.

God is coming after all those things you have always wanted and are now just waiting on the opportunity to present itself, even though you know having them is against his will. He's coming to purge those things out from your heart. Ask me how I know! When God purges us he comes after the pollution and contaminations in our hearts. Before we can get delivered God first has to deal with us, all of our superficiality; it's not the other people with the problem as we may think. It's us. We may not know that superficiality exists within us; there again, God knows.

He purges the heart one sin at a time and step-by-step, and that's the reason deliverance is a process that takes time. Mind you, the time it takes to get free from strongholds and oppression to the place of complete deliverance is shorter if we repent and obey God instantly. The longer we resist, deny, and disobey him, the longer the deliverance process will take.

When the Holy Spirit gave me the instructions he already knew what my response would be and that the process was going to take time. For one, he knew I was blind to the greater deception behind my intrigue and, in this season, he would purge it out. The Lord always had a hedge of protection around me since I was a child. He sheltered me, and I didn't venture out from his refuge. But now, I was about to discover life beyond the shelter, who I was and what I would do. He knew I would repent and get back into fellowship with him, and he already knew he would love me through the entire process.

WHAT TO EXPECT WHEN GOD PURGES THE HEART

My lesson to you as a Christian who is either being purged or will eventually go through a purging is that God will love you through the process, but don't take his love for granted and be willing to suffer the consequences of your disobedience. Stay in his will and do what he says.

WHAT TO EXPECT WHEN GOD PURGES THE HEART

But don't just listen to God's word.
You must do what it says. Otherwise, you are only
fooling yourselves.
James 1:22 (NLT)

Don't twist God's words

My conversation with God did not end in a prayer of repentance. Instead, I had a huge grin on my face just like the Grinch who stole Christmas. I heard the answer I wanted to hear, but I had not heard God's answer. God said, "Don't touch him."

Just like God told Adam and Eve not to touch that one tree in the garden and do not eat from it, God told me not to touch that one person. For me, he was the apple, the forbidden fruit.

I was deceived and believed God had given me His permission to do what I wanted to do. *(God did not say you could not talk to him,* the serpent said, *he said you could not touch him.)* I heard God's words but exchanged them to fit my evil desires. Why do I describe my desires as evil? Because my desires were contrary to the word of God; they were the opposite of what God told me to do. I was deceived, and God knew it. If your desires are contrary to the word of God, then your desires are also evil. Not just mine, but all of ours.

It doesn't take a genius to understand that the word [don't] is a contraction that means do not. It doesn't take a high IQ to understand that the word [touch] means to physically touch something or someone or to be involved in some way. But here is the kicker, the word touch also means to: 1) *communicate with, 2) contact, or 3) hold on to*. Here's a suggestion for each reader ... when you begin to hear God speak, even basic words, write them down and then go and grab a Webster dictionary and a Bible dictionary and sit with those words to study them before you take any other action or make any decisions.

The Bible warns us to be sober [well balanced and self-disciplined], be alert and cautious at all times. That enemy of yours, the devil, prowls around like a roaring lion [fiercely hungry], seeking someone to devour. 1 Peter 5:8 (AMP). As Christians, we should not be caught off guard by the enemy's tactics, but instead, be sensitive to the Holy Spirit's promptings and be watchful and discerning. For instance, if God tells you not to touch something take the definition of the word touch to get clarity for what God is saying and break it down by adding the synonyms in place of the word touch. In my situation, here's how that would look for the instructions (don't touch him).

I was not to have any type of communication. **Communication is** a verbal or written message or any type of process by which information is exchanged between individuals.

I was not to have any contact. **Contact means to** establish communication with someone or receive any significant signal from a person or object. I was not to have any go-between messenger, connection, or any other source or method to convey information.

I was not to **hold on to** this person **or** make him liable or accountable or bound to any obligations he made to me when we were younger. For example, I'll hold you to your promise to love me, to marry me, or even to like me. I was not to hold him to those words or the implication of what those words may have meant in the past.

When we take the time to meditate on God's word, we get it! The Holy Spirit will ensure that we get it!

The Setup

Unaware of the enemy's devices and blinded by my desire, the communication process started before I realized it. Looking back, I call this the 'setup'. Here's what I mean ... I began to run into high school classmates and old neighborhood friends I had not seen in over 16 years if not more; people who knew both of us. Excited to see them, we shared updates on people we knew and we exchanged numbers, you know, to keep in contact with each other. There was no reason for any of us to be suspicious of each other. All of our past interactions were trustworthy and friendly. I talked with three different people on three different occasions, and each of the three had a connection with the person God told me not to touch. All the conversations were brief, innocent with no reason to cause a raised eyebrow or put into question. Before long, guess who I was communicating with over the telephone going down memory lane, just talking, talking, talking.

Everything he said to me, both when we were kids and when we were a teen couple, meant the world to me. I remember one day he said something to the effect that when we get married, I would never have to worry about that *(he was referring to my being afraid of the spider webs between the brick and around the mailbox at my house. It grossed me out, and I was so afraid to get the mail or walk into the house because of the spider webs)*. I **held on to** his words ... *when we get married* ... and I hid those words in my heart because they were precious to me. I was so infatuated with him. I was not to take those words literally, but I did. I can guarantee you that he doesn't remember speaking those words, they were mere words and not meant for me to take to heart.

Now, let's go back up to the paragraph with the definitions for the word touch. Do you see how easy it is to disobey God when your heart is contrary to his will? The setup of running into people from my past, although it appeared innocent, was orchestrated so that inevitably this person and I would be in contact with each other and it worked. This is why it is crucial and very important for every Christian to ask God for a clean heart and a righteous spirit. But, it is also important that we ask God to purge us and remove every unclean thing. The devil will send the very people you don't need to see or be around to work his schemes because he knows the seeds he planted in your life long ago. Before I knew it I was as addicted to this guy as a drug addict is to cocaine. It only took one conversation over the phone for me to get hooked, and I couldn't wait for the next call or the next time I could hear his voice.

Beware, saints! A drug addict isn't a drug addict the moment he digests, inhales or injects his drug of choice; he becomes an addict when the drug enters into his bloodstream and he feels the temporary effects (euphoria or the high) that he gets afterward **and likes it**. Then the desire to repeat the euphoria experience heightens. This holds true for the alcoholic, the smoker, the sex addict, and the people addict. I was addicted to this person before I entered fifth grade. Sad to say, but it's true. Talking with him was exciting.

Many of us are functioning addicts suffering in silence. Yet, we live and have fruitful and fulfilling lives. We graduate from college, hold high-level positions in corporate jobs, live in nice homes, drive fancy cars, get married and have children as addicts. Our drugs of choice may be different, but we are addicted just the same.

But no more, God desires to deliver you from all of your addictions. God wants to deliver you from your addiction to your exes. Whatever is operating in your life that gives you that euphoria or that high you long for in secret I want you to tell God about it and ask him to purge it out. If you don't, remember the enemy is behind its existence and he will use it to accuse you before God as an unrighteous and unfaithful believer. The enemy will use it to oppress you and keep you bound. What is that one thing God wants you to let go of, but you won't or can't let it go? What is it?

WHAT TO EXPECT WHEN GOD PURGES THE HEART

*Create in me a pure heart, God, and make my spirit right
again.
Psalm 51:10 (NCV)*

God didn't permit me to talk with him; instead, he stepped back to allow me to do what I wanted. In my waywardness, I was as stubborn as Jonah and as strong-willed as the prodigal son, headed in the wrong direction and venturing out into the world, like a naïve daughter, to do my own thing.

What was it like to do my own thing? In a word, stupid. That's what it's like to step one foot outside the will of God. My common sense left. Any time God tells you not to do something and you do it anyway, you're on your own and stupidity and regret will follow that decision. It was a time of my most reckless behavior, and it was the most foolish decision I've ever made in my life by far.

As soon as we talked for the first time I could hardly wait for the next time, and all of my pinned-up emotions came out within 15 minutes of our conversation. It was the same type of excitement you get when you finally run into a long-lost friend.

When this happens you talk occasionally to catch-up and reminisce, and then you get back to your normal life. In the beginning, we both called each other. It wasn't just me. But, I was the one who got too attached again. There was one thing I didn't consider or weigh-in, and that was he belonged to someone else and so did I. We had no business talking to each other. We were not in elementary and high school anymore. We were no longer kids, but adults, married adults. Other people were involved. His advice to me, let it go. He had been through a similar kind of circumstance before and knew better; and so his wise advice to me was, let it go. The final result of the matter concerning us was that I wasn't the one.

God gave me time to grow up. My ex gave me time to grow up. But I was still trying to hang on to God, my family, and him - the idol; and that was foolish. I wanted to keep everybody I loved in my life. I was being irrational and immature. I didn't want to feel the pain of letting go.

Truthfully, no decent person wants to be put on a pedestal to the degree I placed him, it's annoying, troublesome and frankly scary. He wasn't my boyfriend anymore; he was someone's husband and I was someone's wife. That truth superseded and outweighed whatever we had going on in the past. Too many other people mattered now in both our lives. I had to grow up whether I wanted to or not and accept the fact that this relationship was not in God's plan, nor was it in my ex's plan. It just wasn't, and that's why God told me not to touch him in the first place. God knew his heart and what was going on in his life. God knew why my problems existed. No good was in it and no good would come from it; I had to let go.

So, this taught me something about myself. From a teen and even as an adult I still couldn't let go emotionally. I realized my issue was more about me and the inability to let go of him specifically. But why? I've met some great people who are no longer in my life and I'm fine with that, we're still friends, so why wasn't it the same with him?

I was a nuisance before I came to my senses. I would go 3-months or 6-months without talking with him and then reach back to talk one more time. Finally, I made it 9-months and then a year without reaching back. During these months, God consecrated me, and I learned to fight in the spirit instead of picking up the phone. I was no longer stubborn but humbled, and I willingly yielded to God.

One night I prayed, Lord, I surrender. My voice was trembling. The anxiety I had been feeling so strongly, immediately left. I felt it leave. My spirit felt lighter. I remember thinking, after all this time struggling back and forth that was all I needed to do, surrender? After that night, I knew if I reached back to connect with him one more time, God was going to hold me accountable. I didn't want to be chastised by the Lord. He had been patient with me and answered all my prayers concerning the matter. I wanted God's hedge of protection around me and I knew nothing else needed to be done.

WHAT TO EXPECT WHEN GOD PURGES THE HEART

God's grace was upon me and he purged my ex out of my system and this time, I didn't resist. When the enemy tried to pull me back to call again, I refused. I stood against the enemy this time, not God. This was the one area in my life I needed to surrender to God and I did. The struggle was over.

For my testimony, I want to share that I wasn't the one for him and there wasn't to be a legal document between us in the future. So why did I decide to share? Because it's the truth. I believed the lie from the enemy for so long, I was determined to not only expose the enemy's deception in my life, but I also wanted to reveal the truth from my ex publicly. I accept the truth and I value the truth. And now that the truth is out and in the open, the devil can't come back to me and try to lure me to believe the lie again. I went to the source and I know better. The devil can't trick me anymore.

What did I do with this information? I got on my knees and told God everything my ex told me verbatim, and I asked God to purge him out of my system. I told God that I accept the truth and the devil was a liar. I repented for not trusting that God had already provided for me what he wanted me to have and that I had doubted my life. The more I spoke with my ex, the more I knew he wasn't for me either. But I had him on such a pedestal I ignored my intuition. Because of my feelings, I was convinced that I missed God's best. Feelings have nothing to do with the facts. I didn't miss God's best, that was a lie and my feelings were contaminated with lies. God gave me a precious gem, his best, my husband.

God is all-knowing. Disobeying him is a waste of time and it's foolish. Although I carefully followed his instructions for every other area of my life, when I didn't pay attention to what God said concerning this matter I was in the sin of disobedience. That, I regretted deeply and repented remorsefully. When God says no to something don't wrestle against that decision. Attempting to go around God's answer won't work, but the result will be trouble and confusion. If I had to do it all over again, I would stay within the boundaries that God set for me, where there is a peace that comes from being in His will.

Fortunately, God had compassion on me the entire purging process. He communicated with me through dreams, most of them supportive but others were warnings. For example, once I dreamed I was driving down the road on the wrong side of the street, headed in the wrong direction. Of course, when I woke up from the dream I knew what God was saying. He wanted me to turn around and get back on the course in the direction he planned for my life. I did, and this is one thing I do not regret.

WHAT TO EXPECT WHEN GOD PURGES THE HEART

> *Be anxious for nothing, but in everything by prayer and supplication, with thanksgiving, let your requests be made known to God; and the peace of God, which surpasses all understanding, will guard your hearts and minds through Christ Jesus.*
> *Philippians 4:6-7 (NKJV)*

Meeting God at the Altar

Altar 1.

During my purging experience, the Holy Spirit led me to another place of worship to receive extensive ministry in healing and deliverance, spiritual warfare, and to learn how to praise and worship Him at a greater level. He was educating me still, and I was in no condition to continue serving in ministry at my former church until God purged, healed and delivered me. It took time, and for the first two to three years I attended this church, the entire ministry focused on what I needed, what God knew I needed. God sat me down from serving in the church to deal with all the stuff within me.

It was here I learned to express myself in worship and I stayed bowed before God receiving healing. Not just for the issue about my ex, but also for other feelings of loss, even my parent's divorce before I was 5 years old and not being raised with my natural father. I had issues with rejection and abandonment, I never cried when I was hurting growing up (why was that?), just lots of buried emotions from birth to adulthood. I released it all at the altar.

Altar 2.

I had an old chair in my living room that became my altar.

I spent many hours on my knees praying into the arms of that chair. Before I surrendered to the will of God, I was in such spiritual warfare that I could barely stand to leave the house. Whenever I did leave, I experienced severe anxiety. Just taking my children to school and picking them up every day was as much as I could handle. Once, as soon as I returned home I ran straight to my chair and fell on my knees. I shoved my whole body into the arms of that chair. There was so much comfort and it felt like my safe place. I remember thinking this is how it feels to be in the arms of Jesus.

I wanted to break the addiction and stop all contact with this person which was long overdue on my end. At times, as I mentioned in an earlier chapter, before I surrendered to Jesus concerning this matter, I would reach back to talk with him just to get a release from the anxiety as if I had to get a fix from drugs. But that only created a setback and I would have to start over again trying to break the habit. The whole time I was in this battle I was asking Jesus to intercede for me and not turn me over to a reprobate mind. Eventually, I became more and more dependent upon that chair. I learned to run to it instead of running to the phone.

That's how I learned to fight the enemy. Every time I felt the urge to talk with him I prayed instead. I don't care how many times I felt that urge, each time I ran to that chair and prayed. I was home alone every day, and I spilled my guts out to God fervently pleading for his help to overcome this thing. But the anxiety I felt was deep down inside of me. I remember one day telling God how deep it was, so deep that I couldn't reach it, and I didn't feel like I could beat it. I asked for his help.

The next thing I know I felt a knot in the pit of my stomach. I was in a real battle, and this anxiety took on a physical form deep within me. It had such a hold over me that I knew I could not break free on my own. I prayed and cried so much that I started coughing and choking. I felt like I was being strangled, literally. I was choking so I got up from my knees and I ran to the nearest sink and threw up a thick, white foam. Then, the coughing and choking stopped.

Instantly, I thought about the conversation I had with my former co-worker who told me people threw up foam during deliverance services at her church. I had prayed so hard that the tormenting, lying and deceptive spirits causing the anxiety left me and went down the drain of that sink. I was delivered. I felt lighter. I was consciously, physically, and spiritually aware that I had had a breakthrough in prayer. From that time on I spent hours on end in my bedroom reading, studying the Bible, and praying.

WHAT TO EXPECT WHEN GOD PURGES THE HEART

As I continued in prayer, the Holy Spirit taught me something new as I learned to live in his presence. He led me to several Christian-related books that taught me everything I needed to know about strongholds, spiritual warfare, and demonic attacks. I also read books about other Christians who failed in their walk with Christ or who had battled with oppression. I list some of the books I read under the acknowledgment section of this book. I became more of an avid reader and spent time during the day with books. I was growing and getting stronger. Each week I read my Bible, a new book, and I learned to fight the enemy's attacks with the word of God. I knew that the only way I was going to overcome this battle was to learn to fight in the spirit realm, and for me, that happened in prayer.

One day while praying, I was baptized in the Holy Spirit and received a prayer language. This took my prayers to a different level. I prayed in tongues daily, throughout the day. Before I realized it an entire year went by and I had not spoken with him. Initially, God told me not to touch him and I did it anyway. This time, I obeyed God. Through the purging process, I learned to obey God. And, to this day, I've never reached back, looked back or desired that relationship again. Thank you Jesus!

FINALLY
THE MYSTERY IS SOLVED

CHAPTER 19

OUIJA BOARD A DEMONIC GAME OF LIES AND DECEPTION

When my deliverance and healing were complete I still had questions about why I had such a strong attachment to this person in the first place. While praying I asked the Holy Spirit for understanding because it didn't make sense to me; no other relationship affected me or had a hold on me in this way.

The Holy Spirit answered my question with one word, Ouija. He gave me this revelation and that was all he said. Very clearly, I heard him say "Ouija" and I pondered that word in my mind. Ouija.

Then, like a light switch being flipped on in my brain I remembered one occasion where I played the game. When I was a little girl in elementary school a cousin and I played with a Ouija board. I may have been in the fourth grade, very young. We were in the den of my home and asked several questions about this young boy who seemed to like me. The Ouija gave answers. It seemed like a simple, innocent game to play.

At the board, my cousin and I both placed our fingertips lightly on the planchette. Then, we waited for it to move to letters on the board to spell out the answers. I mentioned his name to the Ouija and asked two separate questions: did he love me and would we get married one day. The Ouija spelled out yes to each question. I asked the same two questions several times and each time it spelled out y-e-s. I was not moving the planchette and neither was my cousin. We stopped playing the game and I quickly ran to the telephone to call him. After I spoke with him for a few minutes, I passed the phone to my cousin and she asked him did he love me, supposedly while I stepped away. He said yes. She gave me the phone and I asked him again and he said yes. That's all it took for me to believe the Ouija and him. I remembered this vividly.

Wow! I was 37 years old when the Holy Spirit reminded me of the Ouija board game. Before this, that game never crossed my mind since elementary school. I forgot all about it. We only played with the game for 15 minutes, maybe 30 minutes at the most. In less than 30 minutes the enemy tricked me. I was a gullible child playing with an occult game and didn't understand the negative and lasting impact it would have on me. In ignorance, I inadvertently gave the enemy the legal right to plant a deceptive seed into my belief system.

This thing was not an innocent game by no means, but it was advertised on television during the Christmas season as a fun game to play with family and friends. I had a talk with my mom about what the Holy Spirit told me. She remembered buying the game at Otasco and explained to me why she got rid of it. It wasn't in our home very long, but it was there long enough for me to get my hands on it. Thankfully, my mom was sensitive enough spiritually to realize that the game was not of God and she did the right thing by trashing it.

The Ouija board is a Satanic game, it's toxic, and my involvement with it was his entry point; it's how he gained access into my life before I became a Christian. The stronghold created by the Ouija is the answer to why I wasn't able to let this person go, and why I was attached to him above anyone else. The Ouija board contaminated my soul (mind, will, and emotions). In a whisper the Holy Spirit's answer explained how I had been misled to believe a lie, and then showed me how the stage was set to make it appear that what it told me would come true one day, making it easier for me to believe the board without question.

We were two kids who liked each other and who eventually became a couple in high school. The relationship fed the false belief and it took root even within my identity. Our on and off again relationship lasted long enough for me to believe the Ouija board was right. I believed we were destined to be together even if we broke up and dated other people in between. But, thanks to the Holy

WHAT TO EXPECT WHEN GOD PURGES THE HEART

Spirit, the Spirit of Truth, I know better now. We were only meant to be childhood friends. The Ouija board wasn't right, it was wrong. The Ouija board is controlled by lying and deceptive demonic spirits. It is a lie and what I believed was a lie too.

I broke the agreement and the soul-tie with the Ouija board and rejected the [y-e-s]. I stopped trying to make the relationship become a reality. The words my ex spoke as a child and teen no longer matched his words as an adult. I released him and came out of agreement with the lie that he was to be my husband. When I broke all agreements and soul-ties the stronghold lost its power. I came into full agreement with God and his plan for my life, and when I did that the lie lost its power. The enemy has left me alone concerning this thing, and he can never bother me about it again.

But now, just as God told me not to touch him, I'm telling you not to ever touch a Ouija board or anything dealing with the occult. Don't touch it.

***Some people think they are doing right, but in the end it
leads to death.
Proverbs 14:12 (NCV)***

The evil spirits attached to the board instigated the magnitude of the deception in my life. Overall, the purpose was to destroy me. The only reason it didn't destroy me is that I belong to Jesus Christ. Had it not been for Jesus and the power of his Holy Spirit, and his hedge of protection, the enemy would have been successful. I was saved out of the hands of the enemy and redeemed by a loving Savior and wonderful teacher and counselor.

Jesus doesn't want you to be trapped and deceived by these spirits. He's using my testimony to educate you and warn you of the dangers of dabbling in what appears to be innocent games and activities, but instead, they are tools of the enemy, your enemy.

The Occult

Today, Satan is still having a field day using the occult to attract children and adults alike. He uses it to promote false truth. But because you are curious about it, you enable him to plant deceptive seeds into your mind and the mind of your children. You're giving him the approval to make a fool out of you. If you continue with the occult, then you are a willful participant with him. You're not afraid of it and are comfortable with the occult because it's prevalent in our society and socially accepted. The occult is everywhere nowadays, in our homes, movie theaters, retail stores, gyms, TV, and even in the workplace.

Below is a shortlist of occult activities the enemy is using to engage people. Remember, I only played with the Ouija board game one time and for less than 30 minutes and I was negatively influenced by it from that time into adulthood. I implore you never to involve yourself with:

- Harry Potter books and movie series
- Harry Potter games and theme parks
- Ouija board games and movies
- Yoga
- Tarot Cards
- Zodiac signs
- Telepathy
- Hypnosis
- Karma
- Psychic Hotlines

When you spend hours indulging in occult materials a stronghold, an ungodly belief system, of some sort is taking root in your mind. You are drawing evil spirits unaware. I'm not saying a stronghold may take root, I'm saying a stronghold is taking root in your mind, you just don't know it right now. You may not discover it until after many years from now. And, be sure the enemy doesn't care about lying to your innocent children. He is a trickster by nature who targets gullible children. He's an opportunist. He likes to prey on anyone oblivious to his schemes and devices. He takes advantage of any moment of weakness, any innocents, any opportunity great or small where he can get a foothold into someone's life to exploit later for his evil plans.

WHAT TO EXPECT WHEN GOD PURGES THE HEART

The world sees the occult as harmless. But, it's so very dangerous. Do not allow your children to read any type of book because you think it increases their vocabulary, or you think at least they are reading and learning. Reading occult books is not a good thing. Watching occult cartoons is not a good thing. Have you noticed that Harry Potter movies run all day, back-to-back, when kids are out of school during the summer, holidays, weekends, etc.? The Devil is after your children. Protect them and teach them not to touch those things. Teach them what God says about those things.

Take heed because the demonic influence will lie dormant for years, and just when you accept Jesus as Lord, begin to win souls to Christ, grow in purposeful ministry or do whatever God has planned for you, the enemy will try to intervene and stop it (or at least give it his best efforts) by using the legal right you give him. He will wreak havoc in your life and cause you to wreak havoc in the lives of others. So have nothing to do with him or his devices.

Come out from among them and be separate, says the Lord.
Do not touch what is unclean,
And I will receive you.
2 Corinthians 6:17 (NKJV)

Do not turn to mediums [who pretend to consult the dead] or to spiritists [who have spirits of divination]; do not seek them out to be defiled by them. I am the Lord your God. Leviticus 19:31 Amplified Bible (AMP)

> *Do not let your people practice fortune-telling, or use sorcery, or interpret omens, or engage in witchcraft, or cast spells, or function as mediums or psychics, or call forth the spirits of the dead. Anyone who does these things is detestable to the Lord. Deuteronomy 18:9-12 (NLT)*

> *For the Lord hates whoever does these things. Deuteronomy 18:12 (NLV)*

Take back the legal right you've given to the enemy. How? Repent for participating in occult activities and stop all involvement. That's what I did. I have the authority to call on the name of Jesus Christ to expelled anything from the enemy - thoughts, ideas, and images – anything he used against me. Jesus Christ is loving, not only will he instantly forgive you he will also protect you from the danger and all harm that was meant to destroy you. All you have to do is obey scripture. Below is my prayer of repentance. You should pray from your own heart and ask God for forgiveness. He will hear you and answer you.

WHAT TO EXPECT WHEN GOD PURGES THE HEART

Pray

Heavenly Father, I refuse to believe the lies of the enemy any longer, whether it pertains to my past, present or future. In the name of Jesus Christ, I repent for playing with the Ouija Board and inquiring of it my future. I publicly proclaim that dealing with the occult is wrong and evil according to your word. It offends you, and I love you too much to offend you. The occult games give the enemy access to deceive. Please forgive me. I intentionally renounce this occult activity in my life.

I thank you for protecting me and for causing your plan and purpose to come to fruition in my life. I am married to a wonderful husband whom I truly love, and I have two children who have brought us so much joy. You have blessed us, and I am humbled and forever grateful.

It was because of your divine protection that I did not fall completely into the enemy's hand as he sought to destroy me and sever my relationship with you. Thank you for hearing my prayers and running to my rescue. You helped me, revealed the truth to me, and you never turned your back on me through the purging, healing, and deliverance process.

I did disobey you, but I repented. The enemy can no longer accuse me before you as being disobedient. He cannot accuse me of consulting a Ouija Board because you have forgiven me, and the blood of Jesus covers all confessed sin. All the open doors to the occult have been closed in my life and from the lives of my children and their children. My bloodline has been purified by the blood of Jesus. I will never inquire of anyone other than you regarding my life. You alone are the God I willingly serve. You are the God of my family. No one can or will take your place in my heart. In Jesus' name, I pray. Amen.

CHAPTER 20

IDOLATRY. WHAT WILL YOU DO?

Manasseh repented, but King Saul would not repent

The scriptures say that practicing idolatry and the occult is evil and it warns us that doing so makes God angry. Don't be intrigued to know the future. Trust God. Don't worship anything or any person other than the one true God, Jesus. King Manasseh of Judah practiced idolatry and the occult instead of listening to the prophets of God. He was stubborn and God judged him and turned him over to his enemies, into bondage and prison. Later, Manasseh realized his sin, cried out to God for forgiveness, and God heard him and forgave him.

---

2 Kings 21:6 (ESV)
And he burned his son as an offering and used fortune-telling and omens and dealt with mediums and with necromancers. He did much evil in the sight of the LORD, provoking him to anger.

> *2 Chronicles 33:12-13 (ESV)*
> *And when he was in distress, he entreated the favor of the LORD his God and humbled himself greatly before the God of his fathers. He prayed to him, and God was moved by his entreaty and heard his plea and brought him again to Jerusalem into his kingdom. Then Manasseh knew that the LORD was God.*

> *2 Chronicles 33:15 (ESV)*
> *And he took away the foreign gods and the idol from the house of the LORD, and all the altars that he had built on the mountain of the house of the LORD and in Jerusalem, and he threw them outside of the city.*

> *2 Chronicles 33:16 (ESV)*
> *He also restored the altar of the LORD and offered on it sacrifices of peace offerings and of thanksgiving, and he commanded Judah to serve the LORD, the God of Israel.*

Manasseh repented. What will you do? Are you willing to stop worshiping the idols in your life and give your heart to the true and living God? I hope so. Ask God to purge your heart of idolatry. Let him show you where idolatry exists in you. Even if you don't think you have an idol, still ask God to purge your heart of idols. You may be surprised to discover your idols. There isn't anything you can do that God will not forgive you for if you want forgiveness. He forgave Manasseh, one of the evilest kings who burned his children as a sacrifice to idols. With repentance, God will forgive you too.

Unlike King Manasseh, King Saul initially had the favor and anointing of God on his life. But he turned away from God by repeatedly refusing to obey him. In 1 Samuel 28-31, God rejected him and stopped talking to him. Saul became so desperate to hear from God that he went to a medium to summon the spirit of Samuel (who had died) so that Samuel would tell him what to do to defeat the Philistines in war. King Saul once obeyed God and rejected mediums, but now he was rebelling against God and turning to the occult for answers. He didn't humble himself and repent for disobedience. He made matters worse by consulting a medium. God was done with him and chose another King for Israel. Saul committed suicide.

What is the difference between King Manasseh and King Saul? They both did what was evil in the sight of God. One was evil to the bone, punished, repented and restored. The other was righteous, sinned, refused to repent, lost his relationship with God, and died. What will you do? The lust God described that was in my heart was idolatry for my ex. I renounced the idol in my life and repented. My relationship with God is restored. What will you do?

Participating in the occult makes God angry, and he finds it detestable (unacceptable and offensive). Why? Because it is evil, it is sin, it opens the door for demonic influence in your life, and it shows your lack of faith in Him as Lord.

If we confess our sins, he is faithful and just and will forgive us our sins and purify us from all unrighteousness. 1 John 1:9 (NIV)

The Holy Spirit purged my heart. It's finished. He brought to the surface every unclean thing, wrong thoughts, ungodly belief, ungodly desires, ungodly actions and attitudes of my own will, ungodly motives. He revealed all things hidden and impure, and I saw it for myself. I confessed it all before him and I repented. My past is under the blood of Jesus Christ. Neither he nor I remember it no more. I am born again.

I've been purged (cleaned, purified, sanctified)

I am transformed and sanctified, a new creature in Christ Jesus. Old things that were in my heart that God didn't want there anymore are gone. I'm clean. They have no influence or control over my life. My character is Christ-like, I am his representative in the earth now and forever.

- There isn't any lust or cravings in my heart for anyone or anything.
- There isn't any idolatry in my heart. I place no one above God.
- I worship God alone.
- I am no longer self-righteous, but I do walk in holiness.
- I am no longer stubborn or rebellious.
- I am a surrendered servant and friend of Jesus.
- I am no longer disobedient.
- I reverence God to the point of radical obedience.
- Demonic oppression is broken off my life.
- All manner of bondage is broken off my life.
- Self-will is broken off my life.
- Deceptive thoughts and emotions are broken off my life.
- All lies have been removed and cut away from my belief system and replaced with the truth of God's word.

I've been pruned (my soul is rejuvenated)

- I surrender to the will, plan, and purposes of God.
- My will aligns with his will.
- I exist to bring honor and glory to Jesus Christ.
- My identity is connected to Jesus only.
- I yield to the Holy Spirit.
- The love of Jesus flows from my heart to my husband, children, family, and friends.

I have a new purpose

My life is used for God's purpose. I share my testimony with other people with similar experiences. God has called me to write for his glory to lead others to Him for deliverance and salvation. I write as an act of obedience.

WHAT TO EXPECT WHEN GOD PURGES THE HEART

Pray

Heavenly Father, Thank you for looking beyond my faults and for supplying me with a Savior, Jesus Christ, my Lord. Please forgive me for living a life of sin before I knew you and thank you for cleansing me and washing away those sins from my life. I repent of every sin you revealed to me, one by one, all of them so that I can inherit the eternal life that you have planned for me. You have heard me confess each sin and repent for each sin. I have turned to you completely.

I surrender my heart to you. I pray that the precious blood of Jesus circulates throughout my whole body, and as his blood flows into my heart I know it will saturate, purify and change every other part of me.

My heart is new! It is genuine and authentic towards you, sensitive to your heart and available to you. I desire to know you in this way. With this heart, I will be able to love you fully and love your people as you do. With my surrendered heart my priorities will be based on your priorities and my concerns will be fixed on that which concerns you.

I call my desires, plans, goals, and ambitions to submit to your will, your plans, your goals and your ambitions for my life.

Lord, I renounce and denounce every soul-tie that has been in operation in my life. I renounce and denounce the idol. My heart belongs to you.

Mark 11:24 says whatever I ask you in prayer, I can believe that I have it, and it will be mine. More of you is what I ask for.

Thank you, Heavenly Father, for the spiritual transformation that has taken place in my life as I humble myself before you daily. Yes, I decided to stay. I am surrendered to your complete authority in Jesus' name. Amen!

8 BENEFITS TO EXPECT AFTER GOD PURGES THE HEART

1. **Expect to be a new and better person than you were before.**

   Some of you were once like that. But you were cleansed; you were made holy; you were made right with God by calling on the name of the Lord Jesus Christ and by the Spirit of our God. **1 Corinthians 6:11 (NLT)**

2. **Expect to be more compassionate towards others who are in trouble.**

   But the wisdom that comes from God is first of all pure, then peaceful, gentle, and easy to please. This wisdom is always ready to help those who are troubled and to do good for others. It is always fair and honest. **James 3:17 (NCV)**

3. **Expect God's presence to be active and noticeable in your everyday life.**
   God blesses those whose hearts are pure, for they will see God. **Matthew 5:8 (NLT)**

4. **Expect a new way of thinking.**

   Do not be shaped by this world; instead, be changed within by a new way of thinking. Then you will be able to decide what God wants for you; you will know what is good and pleasing to him and what is perfect. **Romans 12:2 (NCV)**

5. **Expect radical obedience to Christ to become your lifestyle.**

   If we have to choose between obedience to God and obedience to any human authority, then we must obey God. **Acts 5:29 (VOICE)**

6. **Expect God to accomplish his work through you.**

    All who make themselves clean from evil will be used for special purposes. They will be made holy, useful to the Master, ready to do any good work. **2 Timothy 2:21 (NCV)**

7. **Expect freedom from guilt, regret, and shame.**

    Now may the God of peace make you holy in every way and may your whole spirit and soul and body be kept blameless until our Lord Jesus Christ comes again. **1 Thessalonians 5:23 (NLT)**

8. **Expect to share your testimony to help others.**

    That is what those whom the LORD has saved should say. He has saved them from the enemy. **Psalm 107:2 (NCV)**

DO YOU WANT TO SURRENDER YOUR LIFE TO CHRIST?

James Chapter 4

Submit yourselves to God – Submitting has the same meaning as surrender. Surrendering your will to God is an act of commitment and loyalty to him. It is a decision you make and a personal choice. After salvation, and as we grow in Christ, we may discover behaviors or lifestyles that oppose God. We then make a conscious decision and choice to surrender to God's will instead of our own by asking God to change us. As you discover areas or behaviors, first acknowledge it before God and invite him in to rule and reign in that area. If you find yourself disobeying the will of God, then you have not surrendered your will yet. You are still trying to control and manage your own life and please yourself rather than God. You will never be able to obey him until you are fully surrendered. Ask the Holy Spirit to give you the heart to surrender. He will do it. He will teach you to surrender.

Resist the devil – Do not allow the devil to entice you and tempt you to sin against God. He is influential, but he is not all-powerful. He can be resisted. Do not oppose God, but instead resist the devil, and the Bible assures us that he will flee. Do not allow the devil to sway you to be unfaithful in your relationship with the Father.

Get close to God – Return to God. Do not be distant. He desires a close relationship with you and your complete devotion to him.

Wash your hands – Don't touch unclean things. Do what is right in the sight of God. Change your behavior and no longer participate or desire what is evil and opposes His will.

Purify your hearts – Ask God for a clean heart and to renew the right spirit within you. Genuinely examine your thoughts and attitudes and put your motives in check. Are you thinking wrong thoughts, what are your true motives behind your actions?

Have a made-up mind – One minute we love God, and the next minute we put our worldly desires above God or put God on the back burner. We need to make an honest decision to serve God with our whole hearts, and not be consumed with the pleasures of the world.

Grieve, mourn and wail – Sin should make us feel miserable to the point where we are grieved and sadden by yielding to it. This type of deep grief and mourning leads to true repentance. Sin brings short-term pleasure, but the end of it is death. When you are grieved about sin to this degree it will bring about true change (true repentance).

Humble yourselves before the Lord – Realize that you have chosen sin over God, but humbly repent. If you humble yourself it puts you in a position to receive His grace. God will lift you and bless you.

WHAT TO EXPECT WHEN GOD PURGES THE HEART

ENCOURAGING AND REASSURING DREAMS

God communicates with me through dreams. This way, he prompts me with warnings if I'm headed in the wrong direction, and he also encourages me when I'm on the right track. Through dreams, he leads me. I've learned our dream language after a few mishaps and misinterpretations. He also approves or disapproves of my relationships, as a way of letting me know who I should trust or not trust. Sometimes, he shows me the heart of a person concerning me. At this juncture, I've learned to be sensitive to him, depending on his instructions, and follow his leadership without question.

Once, when I was going through intense spiritual warfare and anxiety, I was having a hard time and didn't think I could get rid of what was inside of me. I told God I couldn't do it; I couldn't reach that place inside of me because it was too deep for me to reach. The problem I had was too big for me to handle. I remember saying it's too deep and I can't do this. That night, I had a dream I was ice skating. I don't skate on ice and I've never tried it before.

The Skating Dream

I had a dream I was ice skating like a pro in this huge arena. I remember thinking to myself, I don't know how to skate. Then suddenly, I could feel the presence of a person skating along with me as my partner. I couldn't see his face because his chest was against my back, but I could tell he was there and very strong, rock-solid, as he supported my arms during our routine around the arena.

He doesn't realize I don't know how to skate, I thought. I wondered what would happen if I allowed my body to drop. So, I did it. As we skated around the arena I allowed my body to go limp, and my partner lifted me up as if it was part of our routine. It was so smooth; we didn't miss a beat. We continued to skate around the arena as if nothing happened.

The Interpretation

When I woke up I knew exactly what the dream meant. Jesus was my partner in the dream. He was showing me that with him I can do the impossible. With him, I can do what I've never done before, and he is there to help me. He let me know that he is holding me up and wasn't going to let me fall. He is my partner, he is my strength, he is my helper. And, if I fell, he already knew I would and was prepared to lift me up. When I'm up, we will carry on as partners as if nothing (the fall) ever happened. He had my back.

Thank you, Jesus.

The Intercessors Dream

I dreamed that I heard people talking from a distance. At first, their voices seemed far away, but they came closer and louder and very clear to me. The voices were of people praying. At first, their prayers were soft and gentle, but then the prayers became intense and loud. I could hear them praying directly into my ear as if they were standing over me praying. I could tell this was a group of people I knew and they knew me, so I was not alarmed. They were interceding for me and had been praying for me for a long time.

The Interpretation

The voices were the intercessors at my church who the Holy Spirit assigned to pray for me as God purged, healed, and delivered me from strongholds. The prayers were calm initially, but as the spiritual warfare against me intensified so did their prayers. When I felt weak and was struggling spiritually, their prayers for me intensified again. The intercessors were in warfare against the enemy as I was in trouble and couldn't fight for myself. They surrounded me in prayer so I could hear them speak directly into my ear.

When I woke up I knew the meaning of the dream. I jumped out of bed onto my knees to the floor to pray. God let me know that not only was I praying for myself, the intercessors were praying for me too. He wanted me to know that I had no excuse to go back into sin. I could now walk in obedience. The fight was over. The open doors the enemy had to access my life had been closed. I had prayed and repented. Everything I needed to walk in holiness was available to me. The fight was over. It was finished. From that time on I changed. I never reached back into my past again. I never spoke to my ex again.

James 5:16 says confess your sins to each other and pray for each other so that you may be healed. The prayer of a righteous person is powerful and effective. I learned firsthand that intercessors are valuable to the Kingdom of God. They are his first line of defense against the enemy, and I will never forget the sound of them praying for me. I am grateful for their obedience.

This next dream came after my relationship with God was already restored. Deep down, I felt like I failed God. Before I went through the purging process I was self-righteous; I didn't know myself as well as I thought. When I disobeyed God and behaved the way I did, I was disappointed in myself. Even though my relationship with God was good, I didn't feel worthy internally. God decided to reaffirm my identity in him.

The Hospital Dream

I dreamed I was at the hospital lying in a hospital bed. A nurse was taking good care of me, but she left the room for a moment. As she walked out I began to feel something moving under the sheets. I reached back for the handheld remote and pushed the button to call the nurse back into my room. Before she arrived, and to my surprise, I gave birth to a baby. I didn't know I was pregnant. The nurse walked into the room just as the baby was born.

I said to the nurse, "I'm dirty. I need to be cleaned". The nurse replied, "No, you don't." I said, "The baby is dirty, don't you have to clean her up?" But the nurse replied, "No". I was puzzled because I could see the baby needed to be cleaned from the new birth. I asked, "You don't have to clean the baby?" And again, the nurse said, "No". I looked at the baby and the baby began to grow from a newborn to an infant and then into a toddler. The baby was growing up fast right before my eyes.

Interpretation

I was the newborn baby in my dream. God didn't see me as unclean and dirty. He wanted me to know I was clean from his perspective. My childhood issues were resolved. I was no longer that baby, I was a new baby and I had been born again.

The Feast Dream

In my dream, I saw so much food lined up along this huge, very long table. The food stretched from one end of the table to the other end. Many people sat around this table. I couldn't identify them all, except for my close friend from work, Tyna. I saw her face clearly.

It was a nice event, a big celebration. I was comfortable and knew I belonged there so I went to take a seat at the time. After I sat down a man walked over to me and welcomed me; I realized he was the host. I looked up to acknowledge him, but before I could say anything, he quickly said to me, "I'm glad you decided to stay." I responded, "Yes, Lord, I decided to stay."

Then, I woke up from the dream.

Interpretation

The dream reminded me of the marriage supper of the Lamb mentioned in Revelation 19:9. I believe God was letting me know that he heard my fervent prayers of repentance. I had a choice to continue in disobedience or repent, and I had chosen to repent. The Lord allowed me to see through the dream that I still have a seat at that great feast to come. I am still his bride.

The Holy Spirit lead me to this scripture reference for the dream, Revelations 19:9 (NIV). And the angel said to me, "Write this: Blessed are those who are invited to the wedding feast of the Lamb." And he added, "These are true words that come from God."

WHAT TO EXPECT WHEN GOD PURGES THE HEART

About My Husband

Terry knew about my issue. God gave him the grace to love me through my brokenness, and when God began to purge me by bringing up and out all things I buried on the inside, my husband was right there with me, and for the entire time, he remained a true friend and husband. He is an example of the love of Christ.

When we come to Jesus broken, confused, full of sin, hurt, deceived, and lost, what does Jesus do? Jesus accepts us, embraces us without judgment, and he transforms our life. Jesus loves us through our brokenness. That's what my husband Terry did for me, he loved me through my brokenness.

Terry never exposed my secret pain. Instead, he allowed me to talk it out, to express myself, and not once did he hold it against me. He didn't go behind my back to complain to his family or our friends about me. He never threatened to leave or any of that foolishness. What I went through was our problem and we took it to God. At church, I spent time at the altar often for emotional healing and deliverance and Terry was right there, a minister of the gospel, allowing his wife to express herself to get what she needed from God.

Many times I witnessed my husband on his knees praying for me. And, when he knew I wasn't acting right and being rebellious, he reminded me of the word of God. I remember him saying to me once, you know better, repent! Even in his rebuke, there was kindness and love. I needed that. I remember him holding me close one night and praying for me; he refused to allow the enemy to defeat me. Remember, we had been married 17 years before I was purged so he knew the women he married. I had been a loving and supportive wife and mother, a faithful Christian, but during this season, I wasn't myself. Because he understood spiritual warfare, he covered me in prayer, with love, patience, counsel, kindness and rebuke.

That's why I say not to talk with exes about how you feel. You're talking to the wrong man if you do. The wrong man will not cover your weakness they will expose it, especially if they don't have any love for you. The wrong man won't understand you because they don't know you, and they won't allow you to be fully transparent and raw about issues from your past. If I were married to the wrong man, my issues would have put our relationship at risk.

The man I married, as wonderful as he is, was not the person the enemy had convinced me would be my husband, but he was the man God chose for me. I wish I had been healed emotionally before we married or grieved my loss before we married, but I didn't. It's a blessing that God didn't allow me to lose out on a family. And, for that, Jesus I am forever grateful.

Thank you Terry. I honor you in Christ our Savior. I honor and love you as your wife.

PRODUCING FRUIT FOR HIS KINGDOM

Books are available on Amazon.com, both e-book and print-on-demand books

Join our SurrenderNews community on Facebook. Are you surrendering to the will of Jesus Christ? Share your testimony.

Website: www.sabrinamstephens.com

www.ingramcontent.com/pod-product-compliance
Lightning Source LLC
Chambersburg PA
CBHW051837090426
42736CB00011B/1843